W9-CYA-269

F 040990
I.U.S.B.
USED BOOK
$27.00

PROGRAMMING

Programming books from boyd & fraser

Structuring Programs in Microsoft BASIC
BASIC Fundamentals and Style
Applesoft BASIC Fundamentals and Style
Complete BASIC: For the Short Course
Fundamentals of Structured COBOL
Advanced Structured COBOL: Batch and Interactive
Comprehensive Structured COBOL
Pascal
WATFIV-S Fundamentals and Style
VAX Fortran
Fortran 77 Fundamentals and Style
Learning Computer Programming: Structured Logic, Algorithms, and Flowcharting
Structured BASIC Fundamentals and Style for the IBM® PC and Compatibles
C Programming
dBASE III PLUS® Programming

Also available from boyd & fraser

Database Systems: Management and Design
Using Pascal: An Introduction to Computer Science I
Using Modula-2: An Introduction to Computer Science I
Data Abstraction and Structures: An Introduction to Computer Science II
Fundamentals of Systems Analysis with Application Design
Data Communications for Business
Data Communications Software Design
Microcomputer Applications: Using Small Systems Software
The Art of Using Computers
Using Microcomputers: A Hands-On Introduction
A Practical Approach to Operating Systems
Microcomputer Database Management Using dBASE III PLUS®
Microcomputer Database Management Using R:BASE System V®
Office Automation: An Information Systems Approach
Microcomputer Applications: Using Small Systems Software, Second Edition
Mastering Lotus 1-2-3®
Using Enable™: An Introduction to Integrated Software
PC-DOS®/MS-DOS® Simplified

Shelly, Cashman, and Forsythe books from boyd & fraser

Computer Fundamentals with Application Software
Workbook and Study Guide to accompany Computer Fundamentals with Application Software
Learning to Use SUPERCALC®3, dBASE III®, and WORDSTAR® 3.3: An Introduction
Learning to Use SUPERCALC®3: An Introduction
Learning to Use dBASE III®: An Introduction
Learning to Use WORDSTAR® 3.3: An Introduction
BASIC Programming for the IBM® Personal Computer
Workbook and Study Guide to accompany BASIC Programming for the IBM® Personal Computer
Structured COBOL — Flowchart Edition
Structured COBOL — Pseudocode Edition
Turbo Pascal Programming

C

PROGRAMMING

STEVE WORTHINGTON

COPYRIGHT 1988
BOYD & FRASER PUBLISHING COMPANY
BOSTON

CREDITS:

Publisher: Tom Walker
Editor: Marjorie Schlaikjer
Production Coordinator: Donna Villanucci
Director of Production: Becky Herrington
Director of Manufacturing: Erek Smith
Cover/Book Design: Becky Herrington
Cover Photography: Mark Wiklund
Chapter Numbers/Letters Design: Ken Russo

© 1988 by Boyd & Fraser.
All rights reserved. No part of this work may be reproduced or used in any form or by any means—graphic, electronic, or mechanical, including photocopying, recording, taping, or information and retrieval systems—without written permission from the publisher.

Manufactured in the United States of America

UNIX™ is a trademark of Bell Laboratories, Inc.
XENIX™ is a trademark of Microsoft Corporation

Library of Congress Cataloging-in-Publication Data

Worthington, Stephen, 1955–
    C programming / Stephen Worthington.
       p.   cm.
    Includes index.
    ISBN 0-87835-297-X
    1. C (Computer program language)   I. Title.
QA76.73.C15W66 1988
005.13'3--dc19   87-30412
                                                                  CIP

10 9 8 7 6 5 4 3 2 1

Dedicated to the people of Boyd & Fraser Publishing Company without whom this book wouldn't exist, and my family without whom I wouldn't have survived writing it.

CONTENTS

PREFACE

The C programming language, one of the most powerful languages developed to date, was written by Dennis Ritchie at Bell Laboratories in 1972. The language was originally written for the development of the UNIX operating system on a Digital Equipment PDP-11 minicomputer. The early history of C is closely tied to that of the UNIX operating system, but C is now available on almost every kind of computer, as well as on a multitude of operating systems.

The proliferation of C in industry cannot be overemphasized. Most of the modern workstation systems and application software packages are written in C. C is also widely used in communications software, CAD systems, process control, simulation, and even in Artificial Intelligence combined with LISP. Its widespread use has created a huge demand for programmers who have a mastery of the language. Now, more than ever before, students entering the work force need to be equipped with a knowledge of C.

ABOUT THIS BOOK

C PROGRAMMING is appropriate for students in Computer Science, CIS, and electrical engineering programs. The text assumes that students have had experience programming in at least one other language and understand basic programming concepts, such as the difference between variables and constants. This text is suited for a stand-alone course in C Programming, or as a supplementary text for other courses where proficiency in C is important, such as operating systems, data structures, software engineering, systems programming, comparative programming languages, graphics, or computer architecture.

This text not only provides a solid introduction to the basics of programming in C, but it emphasizes the sound programming practice, technique, and style necessary for the computer scientist, software engineer, or professional programmer. The author has also included valuable reference material useful even to the skilled C programmer.

This book introduces the basic tools and techniques necessary to acquaint the student with the fundamentals of programming in C, while focusing on in-depth coverage of the more advanced topics associated with the language. The author has included hundreds of realistic examples taken from his ten years of experience in industry as a C programmer. It is highly recommended that students try as many of the examples as possible on their own systems, since the experience gained from experimentation is the best way to truly become a master of this language.

DISTINGUISHING FEATURES

Development of Tools and Techniques

This book emphasizes the tools of the C language, rather than the "how-tos" of programming. Among the tools in this text are numerous widely-used algorithms including the bubble sort, the quick sort, tree traversal, string handling, recursion, and techniques of modular programming and modular debugging.

Numerous Examples and Case Studies

Many students learn best by example. The author has provided the student with hundreds of realistic examples ranging from simple to complex. Each feature of the language is covered in small examples so the student can quickly try the feature. Additionally, there are numerous case studies throughout the text. Case studies and examples are drawn from diverse fields to emphasize the flexibility of the C language.

ANSI Standards Followed

The materials and examples in this book all adhere to the ANSI standard for C. In addition, the author notes any instance where material or code contain features beyond the original Kernighan and Ritchie standard.

Comprehensive Treatment of Pointers

The author gives a thorough and detailed discussion of pointers; one of the most difficult concepts for students to master. To reinforce this concept, subsequent examples and exercises using pointers are used repeatedly.

Strong Emphasis on Data Structures

This emphasis has a dual purpose. It demonstrates the flexibility of the C data types while also introducing the use of the more common data structures including stacks, buffers, queues, linked lists, and trees. This section will also provide a useful review to the student already familiar with these data structures. Emphasis is placed on choosing the best data structure for the application.

Reference for the Most Common C Library Functions

Many reference materials are included as valuable resources for everyday programming, which can be useful long after a student has become fluent in C. Included in this text are a reference chart on operator precedence, an ASCII conversion chart, and a base conversion chart. Additionally, Chapter 11 contains a reference on the most common system and utility functions.

Review Questions and Programming Exercises

Every chapter concludes with numerous review questions to reinforce the concepts, principles, and terminology covered in the chapter. The answers to odd-numbered questions appear at the back of the book in Appendix G. Additionally, students have the opportunity to practice their skills by completing the extensive selection of programming exercises and projects found at the end of every chapter.

Program Optimization

A major concern of programmers working in C are topics involving program optimization. A whole chapter is devoted to the general guidelines of this important area. A strong discussion is also included outlining the trade-offs involved in various programming practices.

Solid Coverage of Bitwise Operators

A complete chapter is also dedicated to the topic of bitwise operators. Bitwise operators are important to C programmers, because C has replaced assembly language in many applications. The chapter begins with a review of the basics of binary arithmetic and Boolean operations. Each of the C Boolean operators is covered in detail and demonstrated in examples.

INSTRUCTOR'S MANUAL

A comprehensive Instructor's Manual accompanies C PROGRAMMING, and follows the organization of the text. Chapters of the Instructor's Manual include those listed on the following page.

- Lecture outline
- General comments
- Chapter goals
- Solutions to Programming Exercises and even-numbered questions

Included in the Instructor's Manual is an extensive collection of over 100 transparency masters. These masters include selected figures, tables, and program segments from the text.

ORGANIZATION

An Introduction to C

Chapter 1 examines the place C holds in the world of programming languages. A comprehensive discussion of strengths and weaknesses of C is included.

Creating a Program

Chapter 2 examines the basics of creating a program in C. The chapter explains the process of compilation and linking used to create executable programs, and provides examples that cover most situations.

Language Conventions and Rules

Chapter 3 introduces the structure of C programs to the student and provides the information needed to write rudimentary programs. Coding conventions and style are introduced and explained. The student is also introduced to the use of functions, and the **printf** function is covered.

Data Types and Operators

Chapter 4 covers variables, constants, and operators. Each variable class and type is covered in depth. The different ways of designating constants is discussed, and possible pitfalls pointed out, and each operator (except bitwise operators) is explained and demonstrated.

Bitwise Operations

Chapter 5 covers the bitwise operators. The chapter begins with a review of the basics. The use of binary, octal, decimal, and hexadecimal notation is reviewed. The Boolean operations are discussed and truth tables are shown. Each of the C Boolean operators is covered in detail and demonstrated in examples.

Control Flow and Loops

Chapter 6 covers various ways of controlling program flow. The conditional branch, loop, and unconditional branch constructs are covered in detail. Coding for clarity and maintainability is emphasized. The use of **goto**, **break**, and **continue** are discussed with more acceptable alternatives shown.

Pointers and Arrays

Chapter 7 covers the use of pointers and arrays. The use of pointers is one of the most difficult concepts for students to grasp. Pointers are explained in both words and examples. In addition, a set of guidelines is provided for the use of pointers. Numerous examples are provided for student experimentation.

Functions and Program Structure

Chapter 8 provides more depth to the coverage of functions. The difference between call-by-value and call-by-reference is explained and the ramifications of each are discussed. The student is introduced to the different ways of defining functions, and how they relate to overall program structure. Emphasis is placed on clear delineation of each function's purpose. The use of pointers as arguments is covered in depth with the advantages and risks explained.

Typedef Statements and the Structure Data Type

Chapter 9 covers the **typedef** and **struct** statements. Students are shown how they can use the **typedef** to improve the readability and portability of their programs. Structures are covered in depth, with special notes on what is not standard in Kernighan and Ritchie, but is available with most modern compilers. Extra coverage is provided for the use of pointers with structures. Chapter 9 also covers unions and the enumeration types.

Data Structures in C

Chapter 10 covers data structures and their use in C. The student will require some knowledge of various data structures if he or she is to write programs professionally. This chapter starts with the basics of dynamic memory allocation and then gives a synopsis of the most common data structures, shows how they are defined in C, and provides sample functions for manipulating them.

Standard System Functions

Chapter 11 is a reference for the most common library functions. Each function is described, the format of the function call is shown, the legal arguments listed, and examples provided.

Debugging Hints

Chapter 12 is dedicated to the subject of debugging, a topic which is rarely given the coverage it deserves. The student that pursues programming as a career will spend a large percentage of his or her time debugging programs. This chapter gives general guidelines for debugging and examples of special problems encountered in C.

Efficiency and Speed

Chapter 13 discusses program optimization. The C language is often used in real-time applications and in applications with severe memory constraints. Although code written in C is usually quite efficient, the student should be familiar with some techniques for optimizing a program. The various trade-offs between speed, memory requirements, and clarity are discussed.

Appendices

The appendices provide reference materials for the student and the answers to the odd-numbered review questions. The reference materials include an operator precedence chart, an ASCII character conversion chart, a base conversion chart, a reference for XENIX support programs, a reference for XENIX include files, and a list of C compiler options.

ACKNOWLEDGEMENTS

I wish to express my sincere thanks to the people at Boyd & Fraser, especially Marjorie Schlaikjer and Donna Villanucci, without whom this book would not exist. I am also grateful to the following reviewers for their helpful suggestions: Jacobo Carrasquel, Carnegie-Mellon University; Dain Smith, Mount Hood Community College; Mike Michaelson, Palomar College; Lawrence L. Rose, University of Pittsburgh; Laurence E. Kunes, Indiana State University; David A. Smallberg, University of California at Los Angeles; Jeff Mellman, Columbus Technical Institute; and Michael Petro, Cleveland State University. These reviewers were instrumental in setting the tone and direction of this book.

AN INTRODUCTION TO C

LEARNING OBJECTIVES

- Introduce the C language.
- Describe how C relates to other programming languages.
- Examine the strengths and weaknesses of C.
- Discuss choosing a programming language for a project.

Chapter

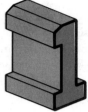

AN INTRODUCTION TO C

1.1 OVERVIEW OF THE C LANGUAGE

In order to choose the language for a project, you must understand the strengths and weaknesses of the languages available. Since this is a book on C, only a summary of the strengths and weaknesses of C will be presented.

C is not a large or complex language, but it is easily extended. It offers the advantages of a low-level language, in that its basic data structures are simple and closely related to the hardware. This closeness to the hardware allows C to be used for programs that otherwise would be written in assembler. The language has the capability for building more complex data structures, however, and it can use them as if they were built in. There are no built-in operations for the moving or comparing of any compound data structures, but most C compilers include functions to perform these operations. The language also lacks many basic facilities such as input-output routines that are generally required. These also must be provided in function libraries.

The C language supports a complete set of statements for managing the flow of a program, including **if-else**, **while** loops, **for** loops, **do** loops, and the

switch-case statement. These statements allow a well-designed program to be neatly structured, and they almost completely eliminate the need for the **goto** statement.

The small size and relatively simple structure of the C language generates some real advantages. Because C is small, compilers for it are easier to develop and easier to transfer to a new hardware system. By driving all input-output functions out of the language into function libraries, the designers have made the compiled code independent of operating systems. To use one system to develop a program for another system of the same hardware type, just replace the function libraries.

The small size also makes for efficient, fast code. The compilers also tend to compile code very quickly. All of these factors have succeeded in making C one of the most popular general purpose languages in the micro- and minicomputer world.

1.2 STRENGTHS OF C

Some of the strengths of the C language in common applications are listed below.

1. **Speed.** The C code produced by most compilers tends to be very efficient. The combination of a small language, a small run-time system, and the fact that the language is "close" to the hardware makes many C programs run at speeds close to similar programs written in assembly language.
2. **Memory efficiency.** For the same reasons that C programs tend to be fast, they tend to be very memory efficient. The lack of built-in functions saves programs from carrying around support for functions which are not needed by that application.
3. **Portability.** Portability is a measure of the ease of converting a program running on one computer or operating system to another computer or operating system. Programs written in C are among the most portable in the modern computer world. This is especially true in the mini- and microcomputer worlds.
4. **Structured programming support.** The C language includes all of the necessary components for structured programming.
5. **Fast compilation.** C compilers tend to be among the fastest compilers on any system.

6. **Support of modular programming.** C supports the concept of separate compilation and linking. This allows the programmer to recompile only the parts of a program that have been changed during development. This feature can be extremely important when one is developing large programs, or even medium size programs on slow systems. Without support for modular programming, the amount of time required to compile a complete program can make the change, compile, test, and change again cycle prohibitively slow.

7. **Clean interface to assembly language routines.** There is a well defined method of calling assembly language routines from most C compilers. Combined with the separation of compilation and linking, this makes C a very strong contender in applications which require a mix of high-level and assembler routines. It should also be noted that C routines can also be integrated into assembly language programs on most systems.

8. **Availability of special function libraries.** There are many commercial function libraries available for all popular C compilers. Libraries are available for graphics, file handling, database support, screen windowing, data entry, communications, and general support functions. These libraries can save great amounts of development time.

9. **Low-level access.** C allows the user to perform some functions at the machine level, such as specifying register storage for variables or bit manipulation.

1.3 WEAKNESSES OF C

Some of the weaknesses of C are listed below.

1. **Lack of strong typing.** Typing is a measure of how closely a language enforces the use of variable types (for example, integer and floating point are two different types of numbers). In some languages it is illegal to assign one data type to another without invoking a conversion function. This protects the data from being compromised by unexpected conversions.

   It is legal in C to assign an integer variable to a character variable, because C does not strongly enforce typing. This is one of the language features that can be argued as a weakness or a strength, but when bugs crop up because the compiler allowed an integer to be assigned to a character variable, the user will consider this a weakness.

2. **Lack of run-time checking.** The lack of checking in the run-time system can cause many mysterious and transient problems to go undetected, when the run-time system could have easily detected the fact that you just overran an array. This is one of the costs of speed and efficiency.

3. **Lack of string and record handling.** This, along with many other similar complaints, may be the biggest weakness of a simple language like C. When a program is primarily concerned with the reading, moving, comparing, and writing of records composed of strings, it makes sense to use a language other than C, which was not designed to work with these data structures.

4. **Not widely used in mainframe applications.** This could also read "Most mainframe programmers don't know C." What this amounts to is that C is not universally popular, and finding people to maintain the program may be difficult if only one person in an organization knows the language.

This combination of strengths and weaknesses makes C ideally suited to some applications and ill suited to others. The primary selling points of C are efficiency and portability.

1.4 CHOOSING A PROGRAMMING LANGUAGE

There is no perfect programming language. Different programming problems require different solutions. It is the analyst's job to choose the best language for a project. This is one of the first decisions to be made on a project, and it is nearly irrevocable once coding is started. The choice of a programming language can also make the difference between success or failure on a project.

In this chapter we will highlight the factors that affect the decision of which language to use as we point out the relative strengths and weaknesses of C.

1.5 FACTORS TO CONSIDER WHEN CHOOSING A PROGRAMMING LANGUAGE

At the start of a programming project, a number of factors must be considered before making the choice of a programming language or languages. The best approach is to ask some questions about the requirements of the finished program, the capabilities of the system on which the program will run and the capabilities of the system on which the program will be developed. Some of the questions that must be answered are listed on the opposite page.

1. What languages are supported by the system on which you will be doing the development? Are these languages fully supported? Have programs of similar complexity been written using these languages on this system?

2. What are the portability requirements for the program? Will it have to be modified at a later time to support upgrades to the system? Will the program be run only on one type of system, or will versions of the program be used on a wide variety of systems?

3. In what languages does the development team have experience? Is it reasonable to train them in new languages for this project?

4. What parts of the project lend themselves to features of a specific language or require features absent from a language? For example, a program which is primarily concerned with calculations may lend itself to FORTRAN, but it probably should not be written in COBOL.

5. Are there requirements for interfacing with assembly language routines? Some languages make it difficult to combine high-level code with assembler. If you need to work with assembler routines, you need a language which supports a clean interface.

6. Are there manpower or completion-time constraints on the project? The best option from a program performance standpoint may be to write the complete program in assembly language, but this will require more development time (and money). A compromise position, with key routines written in assembler and the rest in a high-level language, might prove the most reasonable solution.

7. Is there one language commonly used within the company? If so, using that language will make it easier for the company to maintain the program in the future.

8. Are there function or subroutine libraries available that will cut down on the amount of coding that must be done? It is almost always faster and cheaper to buy a function library than to write your own functions.

9. What run-time support does the program need? What errors do you expect the operating and run-time systems to pick up, and which ones are you willing to catch within the program?

10. What debugging facilities are available? There can be a world of difference between debugging the machine language output of a high-level compiler and using a source-level debugger.

11. Are there system-level programs such as a Database Management System or a Transaction Processing System with which the program must interface? If so, for which languages are the interface routines already written?

The importance of each of these factors will vary greatly from one project to another. It is common for one factor to so outweigh the others that it is the only consideration. It is also common to have no choice at all.

Now let's look at some project descriptions in order to get a feeling for the variety of answers to the preceeding questions.

1.6 CASE STUDY — A GRAPHICS TABLET DRAWING PROGRAM

A manufacturer of graphics tablets is about to announce a new product for the IBM PS/2 market. The product is a tablet that is 20 inches square with a plate sensitive to any metal stylus. The user will be able to draw on the tablet in much the same way as drawing on paper, or be able to trace paper drawings placed on the tablet. Each tablet comes with a controller card that plugs into an IBM expansion slot.

The manufacturer feels that sales would be increased greatly if a simple drawing program where to be included with each graphics tablet. The program must support freehand drawing, lines, frames, boxes, circles, disks, and color fills on an IBM PS/2 with a color monitor. The program should look very professional and include modern features like pull-down menus. It must also support the loading and saving of pictures that it creates. The program should run on any system using MS-DOS version 2.0 or higher.

The program must be complete within three months so that it can be introduced with the graphics tablet. You will be writing the program alone, since there are no other programmers working for the company. There is no further information nor are there any constraints from the manufacturer. You can choose any language or development system that you like.

Let's see if we can answer as many questions as possible about this project and then make a rational decision for development languages.

1. **What languages are supported?** There is support for assembler, BASIC, C, and Pascal commonly available for the IBM-PC. All of these languages are available from multiple vendors.
2. **What are the portability requirements of the program?** The program is required to run only on an IBM-PC under MS-DOS, but it will have to support later versions of MS-DOS.
3. **What languages are you familiar with?** This you must answer for yourself.

4. **What parts of the project lend themselves to features of a certain language?** The program will have to interface with the graphics tablet's controller card and do high-speed drawing. Both of these functions are best done in assembler. The program will also have to perform file functions and offer a professional user interface; things best done with a high-level language.

5. **Are there requirements for interfacing to assembly language routines?** Yes.

6. **Are there manpower or completion time constraints?** Yes. You are the sole programmer and you have three months. This will tend to encourage you to use a high-level language for the majority of the coding, if possible.

7. **Is one language commonly used within the company?** No. The company usually does not do software development.

8. **Are there function libraries available that will help with the development?** There are C function libraries which could aid with much of the coding. There are libraries which contain functions for setting up the graphics mode and doing most of the basic drawing functions. These functions could actually perform the majority of the functions needed by the program.

9. **What run-time support is needed?** Once debugged this program needs very little run-time support. Once the program is released either it is clean or it isn't. It makes very little difference to the consumer if a program crashes with a run-time error message, or just crashes.

10. **What debugging facilities are available?** There are available symbolic debuggers for most languages on the IBM-PC. These debuggers allow you to work at the level of the language with lines of code and variables rather than at the machine-language level.

11. **Are there systems programs with which this program must interface?** The program must deal with DOS. All of the high-level languages listed above can perform the common DOS functions without any problem.

Given this information we must decide which language to use. BASIC would be too slow to support a drawing program, and its interface to assembler is cumbersome at best. The need for developing it in a short time and interfacing with DOS eliminates doing it all in assembler. Of the two remaining languages, C and Pascal, C is an easy winner. The availability of function libraries alone would tip the decision in that direction, but C also has a much easier interface to assembler, and the data structures inside C are more closely related to the machines internals.

Obviously, this example was chosen because it favored the use of C. The next example is slightly less slanted.

1.7 CASE STUDY — BACKORDER REPORT

An automotive parts manufacturer needs a report on the parts that are currently overdue for shipping to customers. The report must be delivered to the president and the vice-president of manufacturing each Monday morning. The program that generates the report will be run in batch mode by the weekend operator.

The program will be run on an IBM 3033. The languages available for programming include BASIC, C, COBOL, FORTRAN, and Pascal. The outstanding orders are contained on a TOTAL database file with approximately 70,000 records. The company currently has over 600,000 lines of COBOL software that has been produced by in-house programmers.

1. **What languages are supported?** There is support for BASIC, C, Cobol, FORTRAN, and Pascal.
2. **What are the portability requirements of the program?** None.
3. **What languages are you familiar with?** This you must answer for yourself.
4. **What parts of the project lend themselves to features of a certain language?** This program is what COBOL was designed for, but BASIC, C, and Pascal also could do the job. COBOL has the advantages of being designed for the handling of text and records. In addition COBOL is widely known, and many programmers are available for coding and maintenance.
5. **Are there requirements for interfacing to assembly language routines?** No.
6. **Are there manpower or completion time constraints?** None were mentioned. It can be imagined that if reasonable progress is not made such requirements will be mentioned.
7. **Is one language commonly used within the company?** Yes, COBOL.
8. **Are there function libraries available that will help with the development?** This task does not lend itself to purchasing function libraries, but there are probably some COBOL subroutines that have been developed within the company that will ease the task.
9. **What run-time support is needed?** Once debugged this program will need very little run-time support.

10. **What debugging facilities are available?** None. Surprised? This is common in many programming facilities. Debugging is performed by running the program, looking at the results, making changes, and repeating the cycle.

11. **Are there systems programs with which this program must interface?** The program must interface with the TOTAL Database Management System. The company has TOTAL interface routines for COBOL and FORTRAN.

This program requires less in-depth study. The fact that it is running in batch mode with no speed or memory requirements, and that it is accessing a database reduces the choice to COBOL.

As you can see each of these projects has different requirements and constraints. In some projects the choice of programming language is simply a matter of taste; in others there is no choice (at least if you wish to keep your job). In some cases there will not be enough information included to make a decision. In others you may not have the background knowledge to make a decision. In those cases you must spend the necessary time digging out the information needed to make the decision.

You will notice that some of the information supplied has nothing to do with technical matters. This may seem strange, but most technical decisions must be made by weighing both technical and nontechnical matters.

It should be noted that sometimes a more detailed specification must be worked up before you can decide on a language. The next step here is to do program specifications to a level of detail that will give you the scope of the program and hopefully highlight any problem areas.

The drawing program requires assembly language only because of speed requirements in updating the display in response to the user's mouse movements, and for ease of interfacing with the hardware. All of these functions can be done in C, but they are easier done in assembler. C is not a candidate for the program which generates backorder reports because there is already a perfect candidate in COBOL.

1.8 SUMMARY

C is a small, simple, general purpose programming language. Some of the strengths of C are listed below.

1. Fast execution speed.
2. Memory efficiency.

3. Code portability.
4. Support for structured programming.
5. Fast compilation.
6. Support for modular programming.
7. A clean interface to assembly language.
8. Availability of special function libraries.
9. Low-level access to the hardware.

Some of the weaknesses of C are listed below.

1. Lack of strong typing.
2. Lack of run-time checking.
3. Lack of string and record handling.
4. Not widely used in mainframe applications.

When choosing a programming language, the strengths and weaknesses of the candidate languages must be matched with the requirements of a programming project.

REVIEW QUESTIONS

1. Why are programs in C memory efficient?
2. What is portability?
3. Why is speed of compilation important?
4. What is the function of a linker?
5. What is a function library?
6. What are the advantages of function libraries?
7. What are some of the sources of function libraries?
8. What is typing?
9. What can be said about a language that does not allow the assignment of a floating point number to an integer variable?
10. What it the major advantage of strong typing?
11. Is C a strongly typed language?
12. Does C support typing at all?
13. Is it generally faster to write a program in a high-level language or in assembly language?
14. What is a source-level debugger?
15. BASIC is supplied with most MS-DOS systems. What is the major difference between this version of BASIC and a language like C or Pascal?
16. Does C have built-in functions for reading a file and printing?

17. Does C support modular programming?
18. What is the major advantage of modular programming?
19. If routines are compiled separately, how are they put together to be used?
20. Is C considered a very portable, or a nonportable, language?

PROGRAMMING EXERCISES

1. Language Choice and Project Specification

a. For each of the following project descriptions, carefully go over the information provided and list the factors involved in choosing a language for the project. If not enough information is supplied, list the items needed and possible sources for the information (if known).
b. Expand the specification to a general functional description of the program with notes on possible problem areas.
c. List the advantages and disadvantages of using different languages for the development.

CASE STUDY 1: On-Line Security Monitor

Your company supports over 300 dial-in lines on its central mainframe. All of these lines are attached to a front-end communications controller. The company needs a program to run on this processor that will log all illegal attempts at entry. The program can use one of the communications lines for interaction with the computer operator and printing of reports. The program is to gather data and issue operator messages only. No action is required of the program.

The communications controller is a common brand minicomputer which supports assembler, C, FORTRAN, and Pascal.

CASE STUDY 2: Furnace Controller

A company is currently installing an industrial IBM-PC to control the process in a heat-treat furnace. The control program will be memory resident during the running of the process, but separate programs can be loaded for special functions such as equipment test or calibration.

The PC will include 512K of memory, a 10 megabyte hard disk, a CGA interface and monitor, real-time clock, 12 analog inputs for temperature and pressure, one analog output for temperature control, 64 110-volt digital inputs/outputs for monitoring/controlling valves and safety interlocks, and a network interface for communication with the factory mainframe.

CASE STUDY 3: Quality Control Survey

The quality control group of a heavy equipment manufacturer has been collecting data on drive shaft tolerances for over five years. The measures of 164 shaft measurement points, and the deviance from the ideal have been stored for each of the 70,000 shafts that were produced during that time. The quality control group has now received a complete list of all failures that may relate to drive shaft problems that have occurred in the last five years. They have hired a statistician to work with you on the problem.

The data is currently stored in sequential files on a Control Data Cyber 180. The company has access to a Cyber 205 if the processing power is needed. The Cyber 180 supports assembler, BASIC, C, COBOL, FORTRAN, and Pascal. The Cyber 205 supports assembler and FORTRAN. The data is required immediately. You should also be aware that the quality control group has already exceeded its budget for computer time for this fiscal year and still has five months to go.

CASE STUDY 4: Order Entry

A company needs an order entry program for its telemarketing staff. The program must allow an operator to enter orders while talking to a customer on the phone. Orders consist of the user's name, address, telephone number, credit card information, and one to ten items. The program must accept the item numbers, read a database, and display the items description and price within five seconds of the operator's entering the item number. The operator then enters the quantity. If the item is available in multiple sizes or colors, the program must then ask for the appropriate information.

When the information is complete, it must be stored on that day's order file. Additional information stored with the order should include the operator's ID, the date, and the time the order was taken.

The system must support up to 12 operators on a DEC microVAX II. Available languages are assembler, BASIC, C, COBOL, DIBOL, FORTRAN, and Pascal. The accounting system and inventory manager which the company uses are written in COBOL. The inventory database is in a custom format designed by the company that markets the accounting packages. Future company plans call for expanding the system to handle up to 36 operators. In that case a larger VAX system or a cluster of VAXs would be used. The company has no plans for changing to another computer vendor in the future.

The President of the company and the vice-president of marketing have both told you that they consider this program key to the success of the company's telemarketing goals.

CASE STUDY 5: Sales Support System

A user needs a simple sales lead database. The program should allow the entry of prospective customers, their addresses, and their phone numbers. Additional information for each lead should include:

1. A call back date.
2. A last called date.
3. A prospect rating from 0-10.
4. The salesperson.
5. A comment field.

The program must perform the following functions:

1. Allow entry of new leads.
2. Allow deletion of old leads.
3. Allow entry of calls made and update last called dates.
4. Scan the database for leads with a callback date of today or older.

The target system is an IBM-PC AT compatible running at 10 megahertz with 640K of memory, a 40 megabyte hard disk and a monochrome display.

The program will be used by up to five salesmen sharing a PC. They must be able to maintain separate databases. Since each database relates to an individual salesperson, there is no reason to believe that the system will outgrow the IBM-PC AT.

The company currently has in-house development tools for BASIC, C, and Pascal for the IBM-PC. Recent development in the company has been a mix of C and Pascal.

2. Top-Down Design

For each of the program descriptions below, write a complete specification for the program. Assume the program will be written on an IBM-PC or compatible with 640K of memory and two disk drives. Specify the program's method of user interaction and include input-output scenarios. Specify possible error situations and the program's responses to each situation. Analyze possible languages for implementation. Defend your choice of language; be specific.

A. *A grade tracking system that will allow a professor to record grades for all of his or her classes.* The program should be able to print student reports sorted alphabetically or by grade. The reports should be class-specific, or it should allow the professor to report on all of his or her students.

B. *An object-oriented graphics program.* The program should accept a file of commands. Each command will contain an object type (circle, square, frame, line, point, disk), its size, and the position at which it is drawn. The program also should accept commands to put the display in graphics mode to show the program, and into text mode to show the commands. It also should accept commands to save the picture to disk.

C. *A graphics print dump program.* This program should dump the contents of a graphics screen to a printer with graphics capability. You will need complete specifications for both the graphics card and the printer.

D. *A text reformatter.* This program will take a standard ASCII text file and process it for printer output as if it were being typed into a word processor. The lines of text are of arbitrary length up to 1600 characters. The program should accept a page width as an argument, and reformat the file for output so that it fits within the margins. The program should reformat by placing carriage returns before words which would overflow the right margin. Hyphenated words at the end of the line should be split if necessary. This will require insertion of a carriage return after the hyphen.

CREATING
A PROGRAM

LEARNING OBJECTIVES

- Describe the mechanics of creating a program.
- Discuss the functions of the compiler and linker.
- Demonstrate creating programs from multiple source files.
- Introduce the use of function libraries.

CREATING
A PROGRAM

2.1 PROGRAM MECHANICS AND HOUSEKEEPING

The information in this chapter relates to the XENIX C Compiler which was used in writing this book. There may be some minor differences when dealing with other compilers, but the concepts are universal. If you are using a different compiler, refer to the compiler's reference manual for specifics about function libraries and linkers.

The process of creating a C program is very similar to creating most compiled language programs. The process of converting source to executable programs is illustrated in Figure 2.1.

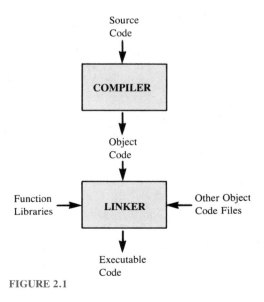

FIGURE 2.1

These steps are required to convert ideas to working programs:

1. Enter the program source code into a text file in a form acceptable to the compiler.
2. Invoke the compiler to process the source and produce the object code.
3. Invoke the linker and supply it with all of the object modules that make up the program and any libraries that are necessary to produce an executable module.

The first function is performed by you and your text editor or word processor. For C programs the source files should have the extension **.C**. This is not an absolute requirement, but it is a very strong tradition. Unless you really plan on being a renegade, you should use the standard nomenclature and get used to it. In addition, some support programs expect the **.C** extension on files.

The second function is always performed by the compiler. This is the compiler's job, converting source code to object code. At this time the compiler will also generate any error messages having to do with the syntax and structure of your program.

The third function can be explicitly started by you, or it can be started by the compiler. Then it will proceed without your intervention. Your intervention is never required when the source of your program fits in one file. However, when it is more convenient to spread the source over multiple files, the compilation and linkage process must be separated. When separate source files are employed, it is your job to insure that each file gets compiled, and when all sources are compiled that they are linked together to form an executable object file. Under UNIX the **make** utility can be used to automate this process. I suggest that you ignore **make** at this time, and look at it when you start developing large programs.

The XENIX C compiler is a four-pass compiler. This means that it reads through the source file four times. These are the functions of the four passes:

1. The first pass is usually referred to as the *preprocessor*. This pass handles the commands which are directed to it. These commands can include file inclusion, macro definition, constant definition, and many others.
2. The second pass parses the C language statements, constructs a symbol table, and reports syntax errors.
3. The third pass generates the code.
4. The XENIX C compiler performs a fourth pass to alter the code for optimum performance.

To write C programs on an IBM-PC, you must have the C compiler properly installed on your system, and you must be able to create a text file. We will start by creating a simple program. The first step is creating the source file. Use a text editor or a word processor to create a file named **HELLO.C** with the text below. The meaning of the code will be made clear later. The ruler at the top of the box is to give you a guide to column placement; don't type it into the file.

```
123456789!----!----!----!----!----!----!----!----!----!----!----!--


        main()
        {

                printf("Hello");

        }
```

FIGURE 2.2

Once you have the text saved as **HELLO.C** type:

```
cc hello.c
```

This can be typed either in upper- or lowercase. This will execute the C compiler and pass the name of your source file to it. If your system is working correctly it will respond with a message telling you the compiler name and version:

```
Compiler Name and Version
Copyright, author, company name, etc.
```

and produce an executable file. In XENIX this file is titled **a.out**. This is the executable code produced from your program. To run it type:

```
a.out
```

If everything is working correctly, you will be presented with the word **Hello** on the screen. The result may be disappointing, but this is often the toughest step in learning a new language. If you check your directory now, you will find that the compiler also created a file named **hello.o**. This is the object file before it is linked with the system libraries to form the executable file **a.out**.

2.2 ERRORS MESSAGES

Try entering the program below into file **test.c** and compiling it with the command **cc test.c**.

```
main()
{
    x=3;
    printf("Hello");
    printf("out there.")
}
```

FIGURE 2.3

When this is compiled the compiler will issue the messages:

```
Compiler Name and Version
Copyright, author, company name, etc
3: test.c identifier "x" is not defined
8: test.c missing ';'
```

The two error messages after the compiler's title line refer to lines three and eight of the program. The first error message is due to the fact that the variable **x** was not defined before use, and the second error occurs because we forgot to terminate the second **printf** command with a semicolon. The compiler will always identify the source file (**test.c**) and line numbers for compiler errors.

2.3 CREATING PROGRAMS ON MULTIPLE SOURCE FILES

The next step is creating programs that reside in more than one source file. In the source file **MAIN.C** enter the program:

```
main()
{
    printit();
}
```

FIGURE 2.4

In the source file **SUB.C** enter the function **printit**.

```
printit()
{
      printf("Hello from ");
      printf("function printit.");
}
```

FIGURE 2.5

We now have the source for a program in two source files. To compile **MAIN.C** without performing the link process, we enter:

```
cc -c main.c
```

The compiler will compile the source in file **main.c** an produce and object file **main.o**. The **-c** option tells the compiler not to invoke the linker after creating the object file. We then invoke the compiler to process the file **sub.c**:

```
cc -c sub.c
```

This produces the file **sub.o**. At this point we are ready to link these two object files with the neccessary libraries to produce the executable. We use the compiler to call the linker in this case. The compiler will skip the compile phase if no source files are provided. The command:

```
cc main.o sub.o -o test.out
```

will cause the compiler to start the linker with the two object files. These files will be combined with the system function libraries and the run-time system to form **test.out**. To run it, type:

```
test.out
```

and you will be presented with the output:

```
Hello from function printit.
```

That is the simplest case involving multiple compiles. Things can get a little more complicated when you need special libraries, or the libraries you need are in different locations, or if the program gets very large. The basic thing to remember is you give the compiler all of the pieces, and you will get your executable file. You can specify more than just the name for a file when issuing the compiler command. Each argument can be a full file specifier. For example, the last command could be:

```
cc \testprgs\main.o \other\sub.o -o test.out
```

which would look on drive volume **testprgs** for **main.o**, and on drive volume **other** for **sub.o**.

Some compilers also accept wild cards for file names. If all source files on a certain volume were part of the same program, you could recompile them with the command:

```
cc -c *.c
```

which will produce object files for each of the **.c** files on the current disk or volume. These could then be linked with:

```
cc -c *.0 -o test.out
```

which will create **test.out**.

2.4 USING FUNCTION LIBRARIES

The following program uses the function **sqrt** which returns the square root of the argument.

```
/* Produce a table of numbers and their square roots*/

#include <math.h>
main()
{
    float x;
    float i=0.0;
    while(i++<10.0){
        x=sqrt(i);
        printf("%2.0f    %f\n", i,x);
    }
}
```

FIGURE 2.6

This program will not compile using the normal **cc sqrt.c** call because function **sqrt** is not in the standard system function libraries. You will see the message:

```
Compiler Name and Version
Copyright, author, company name, etc.
ld: sqrt.o symbol sqrt_: undefined
```

This is the linker's way of saying that it could not find the function **sqrt**. The **ld:** tells you that the error was encountered by the linker, not the compiler. To solve this problem we only need to include the file **math.h** which defines the math functions. A complete list of include files and compiler options for **XENIX** is included in the appendices. Usually, if you have forgotten to specify a necessary include file or an option, the compiler will tell you about it.

2.5 LINKER OPTIONS

All of the examples in this chapter use the C compiler's linker to link the object modules with the libraries to form an executable file. This is fine as long as your program is less than 64K bytes long, and you are not linking to object modules produced by other compilers or assemblers. When you cannot meet these conditions, you must use the system linker. This is slightly more cumbersome, but it is not very difficult.

If your program is more than 64K bytes long you must specify to the compiler that all pointers and jumps in the code must be long format (32 bits as opposed to the usual 16 bits). This is done by including the **–LARGE** option at compile. This will cause the compiler to produce object files that can address more than 16-bit addresses.

2.6 SUMMARY

To create a C program you must enter the source code into a text file and invoke the compiler using the **CC** command. The compiler will read the source and convert it to machine executable code, and then invoke the linker to combine the code with the system libraries to form an executable program. Programs may reside in one or more source files. If the program source is contained in more than one file, each file may be compiled separately and then linked manually.

This separate compilation supports modular programming and decreases the time required to modify large programs.

Function libraries are indexed files of compiled functions created by the user or supplied with the development system. These libraries are a convenient way of organizing commonly used functions. The system and math functions supplied with the C compiler are contained in function libraries.

REVIEW QUESTIONS

1. What is the basic function of the C compiler?
2. How is the C compiler invoked?
3. What is the traditional file extension for a source file under UNIX (or MS-DOS, for that matter)?
4. What is the extension for object files produced by the C compiler under UNIX?
5. What is the default executable file name produced by the linker under UNIX?
6. What is the function of the linker?
7. Can the compile and link steps be combined?
8. How is the linker invoked under UNIX?
9. If the compiler detects fatal errors, is the linker invoked?
10. What compiler option suppresses the linker call with the UNIX C compiler?
11. Does the compiler or the linker detect undefined functions?
12. What option is used to specify the name of the executable file?
13. What error does the linker produce if the same function is defined twice in a program?
14. What is the major difference between an object file created with the normal compiler options and one with the **–LARGE** option turned on?
15. How often should you back up your source files?
16. What is the major advantage of putting source code in multiple files?
17. What is the purpose of the **-c** option on the compiler call?
18. How do you specify that one of your source files is on a different volume?
19. What is the purpose of file **math.h**?
20. How do you tell the difference between an error generated by the compiler and the linker?

PROGRAMMING EXERCISES

1. Enter, debug (only your typing errors will cause bugs), compile and run this program:

```
main()

{

int i=0;

while(i++<10)

        printf("%2d %4d\n", i, i*i);

}
```

2. Compile the same program, but add the -v option. For example:

```
cc -v test.c
```

3. Enter the following program into file SQRT.C, compile it, and run it.

```
/* Produce a table of numbers and their square roots*/

#include <math.h>
main()
{
    float x;
    float i=0.0;
    while(i++<10.0){
        x=sqrt(i);
        printf("%2.0f   %f\n", i,x);
    }
}
```

4. Try compiling the above program with the –M option and omit **libm.olb**.
5. Enter and correct the syntax problems in the following program:

```
main
{
    int x
    x=6*5*4*3*2;                    / just a quick example /
    printf("x = %d",x);
)
```

LANGUAGE
CONVENTIONS
AND RULES

LEARNING OBJECTIVES

- Introduce the C coding conventions.
- Describe the C statement syntax.
- Discuss the C program structure.
- Describe the creation of functions.
- Introduce the **printf** function.
- Introduce the use of special characters in C.

Chapter

LANGUAGE CONVENTIONS AND RULES

3.1 PROGRAM STRUCTURE AND CONVENTIONS

The basic structure of a C program is a collection of functions. A function is a grouping of code that can be called by name to perform a task. A function in C is similar to a subroutine in FORTRAN or a procedure in Pascal. The functions that make up a program may be compiled together, compiled separately and linked together, or drawn from libraries by the linker.

The C language has very few built-in features, so almost every action requires a function. This would create quite a burden if no functions were supplied with the compiler, but most C compilers come with function libraries containing the most frequently used functions.

3.2 STRUCTURE OF A SIMPLE PROGRAM

The C language has a set of rules and conventions that tell the compiler the structure of a program. Let's look at a simple program. Pay special attention to punctuation.

```
main()
{
    printf("Hello");
}
```

FIGURE 3.1

When compiled and run, this program will print the word "Hello" on the screen. The purpose of the individual lines is as follows:

`main()`	This statement names the function, in this case "main", and tells what parameters it will accept. The parameters are listed inside the parentheses. In this case, no parameters are specified.
`{`	This brace opens the function. The curly braces always come in pairs. They act as the starting and ending markers of a group of statements.
`printf("Hello");`	This statement invokes the function "printf". The function is passed the character string "Hello". Notice that the statement is terminated by a semicolon. The semicolon is the only way to end most statements. C ignores white space and carriage returns.
`}`	This is the mate for the curly brace that opened the function. Anything following this brace had better be a new function, or the compiler will be rather indignant.

This program has the structure:

```
program name()
{
        code
}
```

This is the simplest of programs, but it illustrates a few points. You may have noticed that the terms *function* and *program* tend to get used interchangeably. This is because, to the compiler, there is no practical difference between them. In the C language all functions are created equal. The only function treated at all differently is the one named **main**. The linker automatically links the run-time initialization to the function **main**. Thus, **main** is the function which receives control at start-up.

3.3 USING FUNCTIONS

All functions have the form shown in Figure 3.2.

```
type function name(arguments passed to the function)
variable declarations of the arguments
{
        local variable declarations
        statements that perform the function
}
```

FIGURE 3.2

The body of a function is enclosed in a set of curly braces { }. All control structures of more than one line are delineated by sets of braces in C. Of course, all sets of braces must be balanced. Including unbalanced braces in a program will cause the compiler to lose track of the structure of the program. This can often cause the compiler to generate an enormous number of errors when only one mistake was made. If you ever make a change to a working program and are greeted with dozens of errors when you recompile, this is the most likely cause.

You will notice that to call the function **printf** in the hello program, you need only to name it. The "Hello" inside the parentheses is the argument that is passed to **printf** in this example. All function calls must include parentheses for arguments, even if there are no arguments. For example, to call the function **exit**, use the statement:

```
exit();
```

This executes the function **exit**, but passes it no arguments. If no parentheses are used, the compiler will not consider the statement a function call and will generate an error. Notice that the statement is again terminated by a semicolon.

The argument passed to the **printf** function above is a string constant. Any group of characters enclosed in double quotes (") is a string constant. Every string constant must be defined on a single line. It cannot be continued onto following lines. If sets of double quotes are unbalanced, the compiler will generate at least one error message.

In the program example on the previous page, the function **printf** is called, but not defined. This is possible because the system function libraries contain the standard I/O and math functions.

Statements in a C program are always terminated by a semicolon. Statements may extend across more than one line, or may contain extra spaces without causing the compiler confusion. The compiler will not consider a statement ended until it encounters a semicolon. The following are three examples of legal statements:

```
x=3;


hypotenuse = sqrt(adjacent*adjacent + opposite*opposite);


cost-of-product = direct-labor + materials + packaging +
        assembly-charges + interplant-shipping + printing;
```

The extra indentation for continuations of a statement are included to make the program easier to read. They have no effect on the compilation process. The underscore character (_) can be used as part of a variable name along with alphabetic (a-z and A-Z) and numeric (0-9) characters. Variable names must begin with a letter or the underscore character.

3.4 CODING CONVENTIONS

It is traditional to denote control levels within a function by indenting each successive level one tab, or three spaces. For example, the program shown in Figure 3.3 on the opposite page, prints a running sum of the numbers from 1 to 20. The statements within the loop which does the calculation and printing are indented. The loop is a **for** statement with the left brace ({) marking the start of the statements to be executed, and the right brace (}) marking the end of the loop.

```
/* Another very short demo program */

main()

{
    int i;
    int x;
    x=0;
    for(i=0;i<20;i++){
        x=x+i;
        printf("loop index = %d value of x = %d \n",i,x);
    }
}
```

FIGURE 3.3

This program has the structure shown in Figure 3.4.

```
program name()
{
    variable declarations
     code
}
```

FIGURE 3.4

Indenting is also used to denote code that is conditionally executed. The first line inside the brackets, **int 1;**, declares the variable **i**. The second declares **x**. The next line, **x = 0;**, initializes **x** to zero. The next three lines constitute a loop which will be executed 20 times. The **for** statement sets up the parameters of the loop and the two lines following it are the ones executed. The variable **i** will be incremented each time the loop is executed. (A complete description of the **for** loop is given in a later chapter.)

Notice that the code that is being executed within the for loop is enclosed in curly braces ({ }). Curly braces are used to set aside any group of code as a unit. That unit will then be treated as if it were a single statement.

In the example below, the program executes a set of code if an incorrect password is entered. We want the program to do these things:

- Request the user's password.
- Get the password from the keyboard using a user-defined function.

- Check the password entered using the system library function **strcmp**. If the password entered is *not* the word ALGOL in all capital letters, then issue an error message, and exit.
- If it is the correct password, execute the function **main2**.

The code executed when the **if** condition is true is indented to show that it is executed conditionally and is not part of the regular program flow.

```
/* Another very short demo program. This program checks
   a password and exits if the password is incorrect. If
   the correct password is entered the function named main2
   is called. */
main()
{
    char password[10];
    printf("Enter your password");
    getpassword(password);
    if(strcmp(password,"ALGOL" != 0){   /* checks if not equal */
        printf("Your password is incorrect.\n");
        printf("Please contact your instructor.");
        errorexit();
        }
    main2();      /* main2 actually does something useful */
    }
```

FIGURE 3.5

This indenting is not required, but it adds greatly to the readability of the code. In general, loops and **if** statements are indented from the surrounding code by one tab to show that they are a separate logical unit. There are, however, times when indenting does not add to the program's readability; in such cases, don't indent. This situation usually occurs when large, complex sections of code are enclosed in a **while** loop or an **if** statement, and the deepest levels of code start to be indented too far across the screen to fit.

The first line of the program in Figure 3.5 contains a comment. Comments start with the /* character combination and end with the */ combination. This is a little cumbersome, but don't let it discourage you from commenting your programs. Comments may appear anywhere in the program. It is quite normal to see comments standing alone on lines as well as comments added to the end of a line of code. Comments can be more than one line long, which becomes especially useful when you need to comment out large sections of code for debugging.

Let's look at a slightly more complicated program. The program in Figure 3.6 plays the old number guess game. We can describe the program as follows:

- Pick a random number within a predetermined range.
- While the user has not entered the quit sequence:
    Get the number from the user.
    If it is correct, say hooray or something like that and get a new number.
    If it was higher than our number, say so.
    If it was lower, say so.
- Exit politely when the user enters the quit sequence.

```
/*

Number Guess Program

*/
#define MAXNUM 10
main()

{
/* This program guesses a number >0 and <10 */

int number,guess;

number=getran(MAXNUM);     /* Set number to a random# */
while((guess = getnum(MAXNUM)) != 99){
     if(guess==number){
          reward();
          number=grtran(MAXNUM);
          break;
          }
     if(guess > number){
          printf("Your guess was too high.\n");
          }
     if(guess < number){
          printf("Your guess was too low.\n");
          }
     }
printf("Thank you for using this program.\n");
}    /* end of main program */
```

FIGURE 3.6

This is a simple program that plays the standard "guess the number" game. The first functional statement of this program contains a **#define** statement. This is not code that will be executed when the program is run, but an instruction that tells the compiler that **MAXNUM** is a constant with a value of 10. The # in column one signifies a command to the preprocessor of the compiler. These statements generate no code, but affect the compilation process.

The main portion of this program calls several functions. The functions **getran** and **printf** are in the system library, but the functions **getnum** and **reward** must be written. The function **getnum** will perform the following function:

Ask the user for his or her guess. If the guess is greater than 0 and less than or equal to the maximum, then return the number to the calling program. Otherwise, repeat the question.

```
/* function getnum gets the user's guess */
int getnum(max);
int max;
{
int guess = 0;
while(guess < 1 || guess > max){
     printf("Enter your guess, between 1 and %d.\n",max);
     printf("Enter 99 to exit the program.   "
     scanf("%d",&guess);
     printf("\nThank you.\n");
     }
return(guess);
}
```

FIGURE 3.7

The **while** statement in this routine is a loop that will repeatedly perform the following four statements until a number greater than zero is entered.

The function **reward** is broken out of the main stream so that it can be elaborated on later without making a mess of the main routine. The function description is simple.

Give a congratulations to the user with as many bells and whistles as possible.

For the example on the opposite page we will forget the bells and whistles.

```
/* reward a correct answer */
reward()
{
    printf("You guessed correctly.\n");
}
```

FIGURE 3.8

The functions described above can be typed into the same file as main or into a separate file. If you type them in the same file, you can compile it by using the **cc** command. If you type them in separate files, compile them using **cc -c**, where the **-c** option suppresses the linking process. Compiling without linking will leave you with one object file containing **main** and one containing the functions **getnum** and **reward**. The object files will have a .o extension. To link these, simply invoke the compiler and pass the names of the object files to it. For example:

```
cc file1.o file 2.o -o test.out
```

will link the files **file1.o** and **file2.o** and produce the executable file **test.out**. Overall, this program has the structure shown in Figure 3.9.

```
Compiler preprocessor commands
Main function name()
{
    variable declarations
    code
}
next_function_name(arguments)
argument declarations
{
    variable declarations
    code
}
```

FIGURE 3.9

3.5 FUNCTIONS

The functions used by this program are all described in Chapter 11, but you should know that as a general rule, if there is an I/O function that works with the screen or keyboard, there is a corresponding function that works with a file, and vice versa. Therefore, you can expect an **fprintf** that corresponds to **printf**, a **getc** that corresponds to **fgetc**, and for symmetry there are **scanf** and **fscanf** which do formatted input in the style of **printf**. There is even an internal string formatting function **sprintf** that works in the same way. One of the advantages of a language like C, where almost everything is a function, is that it is easily extensible, and if certain features of the general functions are distasteful to you, then you are free to rewrite them in your own style.

The previous program should also give you a hint of the power of a single line of code in the C language. The nature of the language makes for very concise code, where the loop tests quite often contain functions that perform a portion of the loop's task. Other examples of this dense coding are scattered throughout this text, but take a warning: It is sometimes wise to restrain yourself from seeing how much you can do in one totally indecipherable statement.

A traditional program structure can be summarized as in Figure 3.10.

```
Definitions of global variables
main(parameters passed to main)
Definitions of variables passed to main
{
        Definitions of variables used by main
        Body of code for main
}
next_function(parameters passed to next_function)
Definitions of variables passed to next_function)
{
        Definitions of variables used by next_function
        Body of code for next_function
}
```

FIGURE 3.10

3.6 THE UBIQUITOUS PRINTF FUNCTION

You are undoubtedly beginning to wonder about the **printf** statement that appears in all the example programs. **Printf** is the standard output function supplied with C compilers. The **printf** function will be covered completely in Chapter 11, but a quick summary of its use is in order at this time.

The **printf** function accepts one or more arguments. The first argument is the control, or format, string. This specifies the format of the output, and in common usage contains the fixed text portion of the output. The other arguments are variables that correspond to conversion specifications contained in the control string. Conversion specifications are always preceded by the **%** character. In the **getnum** function of the number guess program, the **%d** code specifies that the variables **i** and **x** that follow are to be printed as signed integers. Some other useful specifications are:

%s	Print the corresponding character string.
%c	Print a single character.
%d	Print an integer.
%f	Print a floating point number.

Some examples of the conversion codes are shown below, but first we need to define the variables used in the examples.

```
int x,y,quantity;
float price,length;
char letter,string{20};

x = 5;
y = 7;
quantity = 1100;
price = 3.25;
letter = 'A';
string = "The quick yellow cat.";
```

Given these variable definitions, the statement:

```
printf("The variable x = %d.",x);
```

will produce the output:

```
The variable x = 5.
```

The statement:

```
printf("The sum of x and y is %d.   The product is %d.",
        x+y,x*y);
```

will produce the output:

```
The sum of x and y is 12.   The product is 35.
```

Complicated statements may be written on more than one line as long as the format string is not split. For example, the statement:

```
printf(
     "At the price of $%f per unit, %d units will cost $%f.",
         price,quantity,price*quantity);
```

will produce the output:

```
At the price of $3.25 per unit, 1100 units will cost $3575.
```

And finally, the statement:

```
printf("Choosing the letter %c will produce %s.",
        letter,string);
```

will produce:

```
Choosing the letter A will produce The quick yellow cat..
```

If you were writing a program with the above statement in it, you would, of course, avoid ending sentences with double periods by deciding whether the terminating punctuation was to reside in the data or the code.

A complete list of the conversion codes used in format strings and more examples can be found in Chapter 11. p.221

3.7 AN EARLY INTRODUCTION TO SPECIAL CHARACTERS IN C

Another important feature used in the **printf** function is the \n type notation. The \n is the C representation for a new line character. C uses the backslash character to denote the start of a special sequence that defines a character that is not easily represented by just typing the character. Other special characters that you might need are listed at the top of the next page.

\b	backspace
\r	carriage return
\"	double quote
\'	single quote
\0	null or string terminator. Most functions that read strings will tack one of these onto the end so that you (or other functions) can find the end.
\\	backslash (The need for this one should be obvious.)
\65	the ASCII character with the value 65 (the letter A). This is a dangerous way to code your data. Avoid doing this if at all possible. Remember that someone may try to compile your program on an IBM 370 where ASCII is not used. Not all programmers reading your program will realize that you are looking for the capital letter A.

3.8 SUMMARY

You now have the minimum information required for writing useful C programs. You also have most of what you need to write the main routines for many of the largest programs. Let's end this chapter with an example of the main loop for a large, complex program. This program implements a rudimentary graphics system. Some of the statements used in this program will not be defined until later chapters, but this should give you a glimpse of what a large, useful C program would look like.

        # of columns, # of rows

        data, data, data
        data, data, data
        data, data, data
        .
        .
        type of plot
        output device

If the plot type or output device is not specified, the user must enter it from the keyboard.

```
#include <environ.def>       /*environ.def defines global
                              graphic environment variables. */
main()

{
#include <environ.ext>       /* environ.ext contains the
                              external definitions to go with
                              environ.def. */
int i;

getdatafile();               /* Ask the user for data file. */
if(i=readdata() !=0){
   processerror(i);          /* Read in the data and generate
                              error messages if a problem is
                              encountered. */
   errexit();                /* If there is a problem, then get
                              out of the program now. */
     }
if(plottype == -1)gettype();
if(device == -1)getdevice();

/* We now have all the data needed to generate the plot. */

switch (plottype){
   case pie:
     draw pie();
     break;
   case bar:
     draw bar();
     break
   case line:
     draw line();
     break;
   case scatter():
     drawscat();
     break();
   default:        /* If we ever get here there is a bug. */
     progerror();
     break;
   }
cleanup();
exit();
}
```

FIGURE 3.11

The program in Figure 3.11 is an example of how simple the main routines can be in C or in any other language which supports structured programming. The ideas behind this style of coding are to make the program understandable and to drive the details of the program's operation to the lowest level, where they can be attacked piecemeal. This program is as much flow description as program. In a team design situation, this program could be divided and assigned to the individual members of the programming team as soon as the data formats are defined.

REVIEW QUESTIONS

1. What does the # character in column 1 signify?
2. Correct each of the following statements:
   a. `int i`
   b. `x = 0`
   c. `printf("x")`
   d. `printf("x);`
   e. `if (x == 0) exit;`
   f. `main{}`
   g. `getword("abc,3);`
   h. `printf("This is a statement that will not`
      `       work in C");`
   i. `string = "He said "Hello Sandra.""`
   j. `/* This is a comment /*`
   k. `/* comments can include "*/" */`
3. Can variables be declared outside a function boundary?
4. Why would variables be declared between a functions title and the function body?
5. What characters are used to delimit a block of code?
6. What character is used to end a statement in C?
7. Can a statement be longer than one line?
8. Can text inside quotes be longer than one line?
9. What does the **%d** code specify in the **printf** control string?
10. What is the significance of the percent character (%) inside a **printf** control string?
11. What is the purpose of the **%c** code inside a control string?
12. What file contains the definitions needed for file operations?

13. What do the following character strings represent?
    a. \n
    b. \"
    c. \'
    d. \65

14. What are the argument types passed to the following routine?

```
pocket(num1,num2,num3)
int num1,num2;
char num3;
{
float num21,num22,num23;
}
```

15. What does the **#include** statement do?
16. What characters are used to enclose the argument of the **#include** statement?
17. What is the purpose of indenting code?
18. Is indenting required?
19. How many lines in length can a comment be?
20. What characters are used to surround a comment?
21. Describe the quickest way to comment out a block of code.
22. If **printf** prints to the screen and **fprintf** prints to a file, to where does **sprintf** print?
23. What does the preprocessor do?
24. How are preprocessor commands signified?
25. How many arguments are required when calling a function?
26. What is the purpose of the function **exit**?
27. What is the significance of the name **main** for a function?
28. Are functions typed?
29. What is the purpose of the function **strcmp**?
30. What does the **#define** statement do?

PROGRAMMING EXERCISES

1. Restructure the following program so that it is easier to read by inserting new lines and spaces.

```
/* This program produces a table of numbers and their squares */
main(){ int i;   for (i=0; i<11; i++)    printf(
"The square of %d is %d\n", i, i*i); }
```

2. Modify the quick copy program to remove all spaces from the file being copied. This should only require the addition of one statement.

3. Create a function named **main2** to go with the password program. Compile the function separately and verify that the password program works correctly.

4. Find the errors in the following program; correct, then run the program:

```
main
{
int i;
int j
for(i=1;i<10;i++){
      for(j=1;j<i;j++){
            printf("*");
      }
      printf(\n);
}
```

5. Write a program to print the following pattern on the screen:

DATA TYPES
AND OPERATORS

LEARNING OBJECTIVES

- Introduce the concept of storage classes and types.
- Describe the declaration and naming of variables.
- Discuss the use of constants in C.
- Introduce arithmetic, relational, and conditional operators.
- Describe initialization of variables.
- Introduce arrays and strings.
- Introduce the pointer variable type.

Chapter

DATA TYPES
AND OPERATORS

4.1 VARIABLES

The C language requires that all variables be declared before they can be used. Variables in C have three attributes that are determined at declaration. These are the variable's storage class, its type, and its initial value. The syntax of a variable declaration is:

[class] type name;

or

[class] type name[= initial value];

Where the sections enclosed in brackets are optional. For example:

```
auto float temp = 0.0;
```

declares the variable **temp** to be of storage class **auto**, to be floating point, and to have an initial value of 0.0.

In common practice the storage class is specified only when necessary. This amounts to never seeing the storage class **auto** explicitly mentioned. The type specifier is required for all variable declarations, but the initial value is optional.

4.2 STORAGE CLASSES

A storage class in C specifies where a variable is kept, who can use it, and when it is to be initialized. There are four storage classes for variables in C. The four classes are *automatic*, *external*, *register*, and *static*. If no storage class is specified, the variable is made automatic.

Automatic — abbreviated to auto. An automatic variable is local to a function. When a variable is declared inside a function with no explicit storage class, it is assigned a storage class of automatic. Automatic variables are allocated and reinitialized by the system every time a function is entered. In the following function:

```
main()
{
int total,i;

for(i=0;i<=100;i++)total = total +i;
printf("The total from 1 to 100 is %d.",total)
}
```

the variables **total** and **i** are class automatic. These do not need to be declared as such. The compiler will assume that variables defined inside a function are auto unless otherwise instructed. These variables are not initialized, so until a value is placed in them they should not be used.

External — abbreviated to extern. External variables are global to the program. They must be declared outside of any function boundary, and they can be accessed by any function in the program as long as the function declares that it is using an external variable. This amounts to the variable being declared once to be assigned storage, and being declared again in every function that accesses it. For example:

```
int x,y;
main()
{
     extern int x,y;
```

In this program the integers **x** and **y** are declared outside of any function. This declaration creates the storage for the variables. In order to access them, **main** must declare them external. This declaration does not create storage, but tells the compiler that any reference to these variables must be resolved by the linker, not the compiler. Externals can be accessed from functions compiled in different files as long as the names match.

like automatic

Register. A register variable is really more of a polite request than a storage class. When you declare a variable as storage class register you are requesting the compiler to use the hardware registers as much as possible for the storage of this variable. There is no guarantee that your request will be honored. There is only one motive for requesting register storage for a variable: speed. The targets for this designation are usually variables in functions such as sorts where a section of code is executed many times and one or more of the variables is accessed repeatedly.

In the program in Figure 4.1, which searches a buffer for a specified number, program speed is an important factor and two variables are used repeatedly, the loop index and the target of the search.

```
search()
register int target;
{
    extern int bufsize,buffer[];
    register int index;
    int hitcnt = 0;
    for(index=0;index<bufsize;index++){
        if(buffer[index]==target)hitcnt++;
        }
    return(hitcnt);
    }
```

FIGURE 4.1

Static. A static variable can be either internal or external to a function. The static data class has two specific features which make it useful. The first is that it will not be reinitialized every time a function is entered. This solves a problem that becomes very difficult without the static data type. A classic example of this requirement is a random-number generator. This function must generate a random number from a seed number, and then change the seed. If the seed is reinitialized each time the function is entered, the function will generate the same number every time. Declaring the seed as a static variable solves this problem.

External static variables can be addressed only by other functions compiled in the same source file. This is the only place where the C language recognizes differences caused by placing functions in separate source files. This is needed in cases where a variable is used by a group of functions, but is not required by the general program. For example, the file access routines may all share system data which the rest of the program never needs.

4.3 BASIC DATA TYPES

When declaring a variable, you must specify the data type and the variable's name. The basic data types are:

int   Integer. A whole number.
float   A floating point (real) number.
char   An ASCII character on most machines and compilers. This may be an EBCDIC on an IBM mainframe system.

The format of a data declaration is:

```
type name1[,name2,name3, ...];
```

You can include as many variable names as you wish with a type declaration. Some examples of type declarations are:

```
int x,y,z;
char letter;
float windspeed,direction;
```

Declaring multiple variables on a line makes for more concise code, but is harder to modify later. The most readable programs group the declarations by type or by function.

In addition there are the following variations on the basic variable types:

double   A double precision floating point number.
short   A 16-bit integer. This is the same as an int on most machines. The difference occurs on machines with larger word sizes such as 32 or 64 bits. On such machines a normal word-sized int is not needed for many applications, and a short can be used instead.
long   A 32-bit integer.
unsigned A 16-bit integer that is always positive.

The **short** and **long** type integers may vary between compilers, but for the IBM-PC a **short** integer is usually 16 bits and a **long** 32 bits. The **double** is used where more accuracy is required than can be achieved using a 32-bit floating point number.

4.4 VARIABLE NAMES

Variable names can be made up of one or more letters and numbers and can include the underline character (_). The rules governing legal variable names are:

1. The first character of a variable name must be a letter, either lowercase (a-z) or uppercase (A-Z).
2. Uppercase letters (A-Z) and lowercase letters (a-z) are different. Therefore, the variable names Boston and boston identify two distinct variables. Be careful, this difference may not be obvious to someone reading the program.
3. Traditionally, variable names are made up of lowercase letters, numbers, and the underline character. Uppercase characters are generally not used in variable names. Defined constants, however, are traditionally made up of all uppercase characters. For example, a graphics program may have a variable **color** and a constant **YELLOW**. The distinction between these two would be obvious to an experienced C programmer. These are not hard and fast rules, and they are not policed by the compiler, but they are good coding practices.
4. The number of characters which are significant in identifying a variable vary between compilers, but you can be assured of at least eight. If you are not sure of the limits, or if the program may be used on different systems, restrict yourself to eight characters for variable and function names. You should also be aware that the number of significant characters allowed may not be a factor of the compiler, but it may be limited by the systems linker which must handle all of the external variable names and all of the function names. So as a general rule it is best to limit names to eight characters for portability.
5. Make variable names meaningful, both to yourself and future programmers. Standardize when and how you use abbreviations. For example, if you abbreviate the variable **letter** to **let**, don't later abbreviate **number** to **nmbr**, be consistant and use **num**.
6. Certain words are reserved for the compiler's use. These reserved words cannot be used as variable or function names. These words are:

int	char	float	double	extern
long	short	struct	unsigned	auto
register	typedef	static	goto	return
sizeof	break	if	else	continue
for	while	do	switch	case
default	entry	union		

4.5 ASSIGNMENT STATEMENTS

The purpose of an assignment statement is to set a variable to a value. The simplest form of assignment takes the following form:

variable = expression;

For example:

```
x = 3;
x = getnum(file);
x = 27 * sqrt(getran(maxnum));
```

sets the variable **x** to the value 3. Multiple variables can also be assigned a value within one statement. The following example sets the variables **x**, **y**, and **z** all to 0:

```
x = y = z = 0;
```

In C it is legal to mismatch types when assigning values to a variable. Some compilers will warn you that you are mismatching data types, and the **lint** program will always flag these when asked. For example:

```
int mileage;
mileage = 50.5/3.5;
```

or

```
int number;
char ch;

ch = number;
```

In C there is a special assignment statement for assignments that take the following form:

```
x = x + 5;
```

This is one of the most common statement types. In C this can be written in the following way:

```
x += 5;
```

This form can be used for any arithmetic operator which takes a left and a right operand. This form is especially useful when the variable is long or complicated and you do not wish to retype it on both sides of the equals sign. The operators are covered in more detail later in this chapter.

4.6 CONSTANTS

The flip side of variables consists of constants. The numeric constants seem very simple, but there are some surprises. The number 12 is naturally an integer and the number 5.7 is naturally a float, but what is 3/5? The answer, if you write it like that, is 0, because 3/5 is an integer expression. This can be devastating to a well-designed formula. The solution is to write the fraction as 3.0/5.0. The decimal points in the constants notify the compiler that the constant is floating point.

C also supports octal and hexadecimal constants. Any integer constant preceded by the number 0 is considered to be octal. The constant 014 has a decimal value of 12. Any integer constant prefixed by a 0x is considered hexadecimal. Some examples of the three ways of representing integers are listed below:

Octal	Hex	Decimal
023	0x13	19
0777	0x1FF	511
077	0x3F	63
01	0x01	1

FIGURE 4.2

Floating point constants can be written either explicitly, or in scientific notation. Some examples of floating point numbers and their equivalents are shown in Figure 4.3.

12.3	12.3	decimal
127.32	127.32	decimal
.12732e3	127.32	decimal
12.	12	decimal
.123e5	12300	decimal
.123E5	12300	decimal
123e-3	.123	decimal

FIGURE 4.3

Character constants are written within single quotes ('). The double quote ('') is reserved for defining strings. The statement:

```
c = 'A';
```

sets the variable **c** to an ASCII letter A. Some characters that cannot be typed in normal source have special codes. Although these codes look like multiple characters, each represents just one character. Some of these were introduced with the **printf** function in the previous chapter, and all can be used within the **printf** format string or any other character string. They are:

'\n'	newline character
'\b'	backspace
'\r'	carriage return
'\t'	horizontal tab
'\v'	vertical tab
'\f'	formfeed character
'\"'	double quote
'\''	single quote
'\0'	end of string (NUL character)
'\\'	backslash
'\65'	the ASCII character with the value 65 (letter A).

FIGURE 4.4

4.7 ARITHMETIC OPERATORS

The argument side of an assignment variable may contain more complicated statements. The basic *arithmetic* operators are + for addition, – for subtraction, * for multiplication, and / for division. The following are examples of more complicated assignment statements:

```
int mileage,temperature;
float mpg,pressure;
mileage = 27+12*16;
mpg = mileage/12.6;
pressure = temperature * 11.2;
```

In the first example, the variable **mileage** is set to a value of 219, not 624. This is because the * and / operators have a higher precedence than the + and – operators. This means that if a statement contains both types of operators, then the * and / operations will be performed first. If you wanted the addition to be performed first, the statement would need to be written:

```
mileage = (27+12)*16;
```

The operation inside the parentheses is performed first, and the result is then used in the multiplication. A complete table of precedence is included in Appendix A. In general, operations of equal precedence are performed from left to right. Exceptions to that rule are mostly operators with single arguments. If you have doubts, check the appendix.

The % operator performs the modulus operation. The result of this operation is the remainder when the first argument is divided by the second. For example:

```
x = 21 % 10
```

causes the variable x to be set to the remainder of 21 / 10 or the number 1. This operation is read as 21 modulo 10.

Assignment statements have a value. Therefore, a statement like the following:

```
totalmiles = (driver1 = sfmiles * 3) + (driver2 = 275);
```

can be used to calculate values for the variables **driver1**, **driver2**, and **totalmiles** all in one statement. This property of assignment expressions is used widely in loop tests. In the previous chapter we used this property in the statement while loops of the number guess, file copy, and graphics programs. The statements all take a form like the following:

```
while ((variable = getdata function) != end condition)
```

This allows the testing of data as it is retrieved. As an example, let's write a simple routine which copies data being entered from the keyboard into a file. The program terminates when the escape key is pressed.

```c
#include <stdio.h>
#define ESC 27;

main();
{
char c;
FILE *file;
file = fopen("test","w");

while(c=getchar() != ESC)putc(c,file);

fclose(file);
}
```

FIGURE 4.5

This program starts by including the file **stdio.h** which contains the necessary system definitions for file access. The variable **file** is defined as a pointer to a file information table. This special data type is defined in **stdio.h**. After the file is opened, one line copies all typed data into the file until the escape character is pressed.

4.8 INCREMENT AND DECREMENT OPERATORS

The C language contains special *arithmetic* operators for incrementing and decrementing variables. To increment the variable **x**, simply use the following:

```
x++;
```

or

```
++x;
```

To decrement the variable, simply use the following:

```
x--;
```

or

```
--x;
```

When executed alone as a statement it doesn't matter if the operator is before or after the variable. However, it makes a big difference when the operator is part of an expression where the result is being used. For example:

```
x = 5;
y = x++;
```

yields a different result than:

```
x = 5;
y = ++x;
```

In both cases the final value of the variable **x** is 6, but in the first case the final value of the variable **y** is 5, and in the second the final value of **y** is 6. When the operator is after the variable, the value of the variable is used before the operation is performed. When the operator prefixes the variable, the operation is performed, then the new value is used in the calculation.

This fact is heavily used by C programmers, and misreading a statement can cause dire consequences. The following two examples will illustrate these differences. Both of the following routines count the characters in the string s.

Example 1

Find length of string s

```
charcount(s)
char s[];
{
     int i=0;
     while(s[i++] != '\0'){}
     return(i);
}
```

Example 2

Find length of string s

```
charcount(s)
char s[];
{
     int i=0;
     while(s[++i] != '\0'){}
     return(i);
}
```

FIGURE 4.6

These two routines are only slightly different, but the differences can cause major difficulties. The first example will look at each successive element of the array **s** starting with element 0 and continuing until the end-of-line character is found. The problem with this example is that the variable **i** will then equal the string length + 1.

The second example will perform a similar function and return the correct string length in **i**, but what happens if the string being checked is empty? The second loop never looks at element 0 because **i** is incremented before it is evaluated. Both of these problems can be remedied, though. The two examples on the following pages are corrected for their respective errors.

Example 1

> *corrected — Find length of string s*

```
charcount(s)
char s[];
{
    int i=0;
    while(s[i++] != '\0'){}
    return(i-1);
}
```

Example 2

> *corrected — Find length of string s*

```
charcount(s)
char s[];
{
    int i=-1;
    while(s[++i] != '\0'){}
    return(i);
}
```

FIGURE 4.7

These simple examples, such as + +s and s+ +, highlight where differences between code can cause difficulties. When choosing the form of an increment or decrement operator, always look at the endpoints of the loop involved. The endpoints are where problems are most likely to occur.

4.9 RELATIONAL AND CONDITIONAL OPERATORS

In addition to the arithmetic operators, there are the *relational* operators. There are no restrictions in C on the use of relational operators within assignment statements. The relational operators are >, <, > =, < =, = =, and ! = for testing whether the first argument is greater than (>), less than (<), greater than or equal to (> =), less than or equal to (< =), equal to(= =), or not equal to(! =) the second argument. The most common use of these operators occurs in the conditional expressions within **if** and loop statements. For example:

```
if(x < 3)exit();

while(x != 0)

if( x == y)return(-1);
```

Note that the equality test operator, = =, is different from the assignment operator, =. Confusing these two operators is a very common mistake, and it will not be picked up by the compiler. There is nothing wrong with the following statement:

```
if(x = y)return(x);
```

but it is very different from:

```
if (x == y)return(x);
```

The first assigns the value of **y** to **x** and returns if it is nonzero. The second checks if **x** is equal to **y** and returns if they are equal.

Relational operators can also be used to assign a *logical value* to a variable. A logical value can be best described as having two states, true and false. This variable can later be used in a test statement or as an argument in a statement which yields another logical value as an answer. For example:

```
x = y > z
```

will yield a value of TRUE, or 1, if **y** is greater than **z** and a value of FALSE, or 0, if **y** is not greater than **z**. In addition to these relational operators there is a relational **and** (&&) and a relational **or** (¦¦) test. The statement below:

```
if(X == 3 && y == 5)return();
```

would be read if **x** equals 3 *and* **y** equals 5. If both of those conditions are true, the statement following will be executed. If either is false the statement will not be executed. The statement below:

```
if (x == 3 ¦¦ y == 5)return();
```

is read if **x** equals 3 *or* **y** equals 5. In this case the **return** will be executed if either one (or both) of those conditions is true.

The last type of relational operator is the negating operator !. This operator works on only one argument is used in statements such as the following, which will cause the **return** to be executed if **x** is *not true*.

```
if (!x)return();
```

4.10 ARRAYS AND STRINGS

Defining an array in C is simply a matter of appending the array size onto the name in the declaration. The statement:

```
int x[20];
```

defines an integer array named **x** with 20 elements. The first element in an array is numbered 0. Therefore, the array **x** consists of elements 0,1,2...19. Addressing an element of an array is simple. The following statement sets the variable **y** to the value of element 3 of the array **x**:

```
y = x[3];
```

A common type of array is the array of characters commonly referred to as a *string*. A string is an array of characters terminated by the NUL character. A string constant is defined by surrounding one or more ASCII characters or character constants by double quotes ("). Some examples of strings are:

```
"This is a character string"
"THIS IS ALL CAPS"
"a"
"String with a Newline at the end.\n"
"0123456789"
```

These strings are all arrays of characters and can be addressed as such. The compiler automatically adds the NUL character to the end of a string at compile time. Since the compiler adds the NUL character, arrays must be sized with an extra element to hold it. For example, the string "0123456789" requires an array 11 elements long for storage.

4.11 INITIALIZATION

Variables can be initialized either at the time of their declaration, or explicitly in executable code. Initializing at declaration is done by adding an = and a value after the variable name. For example:

```
int a = 10;
char c = 'A';
float y = 3.754;
float n = 0;
```

This is much more compact than:

```
int a;
char c;
float y,n;
a = 10;
c = 'A';
y = 3.754;
n = 0;
```

Initialization becomes a little more complicated as the variables grow more complex. To initialize arrays at declaration, you must specify more than one value. This is done by creating a list of values enclosed in braces.

```
int a[5] = {3,7,6,5,1};
char message[5] = {'H','E','L','P','\0'};
```

There is a shorthand for initializing character arrays. The variable **message** could have been initialized by the following:

```
char message[5] = "HELP";
```

To further ease the use of strings, some compilers allow the size of the array to be omitted. The compiler will then compute the array's size by counting the initializers. So the initialization of **message** becomes the folllowing:

```
char message[] = "HELP";
```

which places most of the work on the compiler. Try this with your compiler. If you do not get an error message at compile time, it is legal.

Initialization of automatic variables can include any legal expression as long as all elements of the expression are previously defined.

4.12 POINTERS

We will only briefly touch on *pointers* at this time, since a whole chapter is dedicated to them later. Pointers are different from most data types in C. A pointer must be associated with some other data type. You can have an integer pointer, a float pointer, or even a pointer pointer. Pointers are nothing more than an address, but they have some very useful features.

To declare a pointer use the form:

```
type *name;
```

For example:

```
int *bufptr;
```

creates a pointer that points to integers. The pointer itself is not being declared as an integer. Since pointers are most often used in relation to arrays, let's look at a few examples.

```
char linebuf[81];
```

creates a buffer that can hold up to an 80-character line.

```
char *bufptr;
```

creates a pointer to character variables. It does not point to anything when declared.

```
bufptr = linebuf;
```

This sets the pointer **bufptr** to the address of the beginning of the array **linebuf**. This could also be done with the following statement:

```
bufptr = &linebuf[0];
```

The operator **&** should be read as "the address of." Hence, we just set **bufptr** to "the address of" **linebuf[0]**. In C, incrementing a pointer does not necessarily change the address by one byte or one word, but changes the address to point to the next variable in the array, regardless of the variable's type. Now:

```
nextchar = *bufptr++;
```

will cause the contents of the first element of **linebuf** to be copied into **nextchar** and will also set **bufptr** to point to the second element of the array.

4.13 CONDITIONAL ASSIGNMENT OPERATORS

One of the most common expression sequences in programming takes the form of an **if-else** with a variable being assigned a different value depending on the truth of the *condition* inside the **if** statement. For example

```
if(var1 > var2)

        max = var1;

else

        max = var2;
```

This sets the variable **max** to the maximum of the variables **var1** and **var2**. C contains a shorthand expression for this sequence. The same effect can be realized by the following statement:

```
max = (var1>var2) ? var1:var2;
```

This is much shorter. It constitutes only a single expression, so that it has a value. For example, you can call a function with the greater of the two variables by simply using the whole expression as the function argument.

```
plotmax((var1>var2)?var1:var2);
```

will pass the value of **var1** or **var2**, whichever is greater, to the function **plotmax**. It should be noted that many compilers generate the same amount of code for the expanded and the shorthand form.

4.14 AN EXAMPLE

The example at the top of the next page, calculates the straight-line distance between points in three dimensions from the changes in coordinate positions. This type of program is useful for calculating distances when the information available is in the form of maps or plans which give the Cartesian components. All calculations and printing are done in floating point.

```
/* A three dimensional walk program.  The user enters
x, y, and z distances.  The program calculates the new
position, distance traveled on this leg (assuming the
straight line was taken from the last point), and total
distance traveled.  This program never exits. */

#include <math.h>
float movex,movey,movez;
main()
{
        extern float movex,movey,movez;

        int curmove = 0;
        float curx = 0;
        float cury = 0;
        float curz = 0;
        float curdist = 0;
        float totdist = 0;
        for(;;){                  /* This means loop forever. */
                getmove(++curmove);
                curdist = sqrt(movex*movex+movey*movey+movez*movez);
                curx += movex;
                cury += movey;
                curz += movez;
                totdist += curdist;
                printf("You traveled %f units from your last location.\n",
                        curdist);
                printf("You are currently at location X = %f, Y= %f, Z = %f.\n",
                        curx,cury,curz);
                printf("You have traveled a total of %f units this trip.\n\n",
                        totdist);
                ]
}
getmove(move)
int move;
{
        extern float movex,movey,movez;

        printf("Enter the distance traveled along the X axis.  ");
        scanf("%f",&movex);
        printf("Enter the distance traveled along the Y axis.  ");
        scanf("%f",&movey);
        printf("Enter the distance traveled along the Z axis.  ");
        scanf("%f",&movez);
}
```

FIGURE 4.8

You will notice that the file **math.h** is included at the start of the program. This file includes the necessary definitions for using the math routines. This is required since we use the function **sqrt**. If the source is in file **calc.c**, the compile command is:

```
cc calc.c -o calc.out
```

The system will link in all of the necessary floating point routines. On some compilers a library has to be explicitly specified for the math routines. In that case the option **-lname** must be added, where **name** is the name of the library.

4.15 SUMMARY

All variables must be declared before they are used in C. A variable in C has a class and a type associated with it. The four classes are automatic, external, register, and static. The data types are integer, floating point, and character. Variable names can include letters, numbers and the underline character. Arrays are defined by specifying the number of elements inside square brackets ([ ]).

Constants in C can be integer, floating point, or character. A floating point constant is defined as any numeric constant that contains a decimal point. Integer constants can be entered in decimal, octal, or hexadecimal. Single character constants are defined using single quotes (’), strings of characters are defined using double quotes (”).

The arithmetic operators are summarized in Figure 4.9.

+ +	increment
--	decrement
*	multiply
/	divide
%	modulus
+	addition
-	subtraction

FIGURE 4.9

The relational operators are summarized in Figure 4.10 on the following page.

<	less than
>	greater than
< =	less than or equal
> =	greater than or equal
= =	equal (relational comparison, not assignment)
! =	not equal
? :	conditional assignment

FIGURE 4.10

The assignment operator in C is = . This can be combined with the arithmetic operators to form compound operators such as + = . This is a short term way of performing an operation on a variable and placing the result in the same variable.

REVIEW QUESTIONS

1. What are the four data classes in C?
2. What is the default data class?
3. What is the abbreviation used for declaring a variable external?
4. Does the register declaration guarantee that a variable will be stored in registers during use?
5. What are the three basic data types?
6. Which of the following variable names are legal?
   a. integrand
   b. interest%
   c. huge car
   d. hmo345
   e. AlpQ1
   f. A_Long_Trip
   g. 1st
   h. PART1
   i. plan#
   j. far_12
   k. test_bank_number
   l. RECORD_NAME
   m. am-32
   n. Paul's_number

    o. number_of_cats
    p. switch
    q. size_of_storm
    r. COMPOST
    s. CAR(3)
    t. result
    u. _what

7. Express the groups of statements below in a more compact form.
    a. int x;
       int y;
    b. int x;
       x = 3;
    c. x = 0;
       y = 0;
    d. x = x + y;
    e. int x,y;
       x = y - (y/10)*10;
    f. x = x + 1;
    g. x += 1;
    h. y = x;
       --x;

8. What is the effect of the modifier **double** in the declaration below?

    double float max;

9. What are the variations that can be added to the basic data types?
10. What is the effect of the modifier **unsigned** on an integer?
11. How do you insure that a constant is of type float?
12. What are the values of the following expressions?
    a. 13.3 + 7/10
    b. (7 < 10)
    c. '\\'
    d. '\n'
    e. '\''
    f. .3E1
    g. 022
    h. 0x22
    i. 22
13. What is suspicious about the following statement?

    if(x = y)plotx();

14. What is the value of **y** after the following sequence?

```
x = 3;
y = (x>3);
```

15. What is wrong with the following sequence?

```
int x[20];
x[20] = 5;
```

16. How large will the array **password** be in the line below?

```
char password[] = "liberty";
```

17. What is the final value of **x** in the sequence below?

```
x = y = z = 2;
z = Y-- * x;
x = (x != y ) ? z : y;
```

18. What is the final value of **y** in the sequence below?

```
float y;
int x;
y = 3.54;
x = y;
y = x;
```

19. Which of the following are reserved words in C?
    a. double
    b. then
    c. while
    d. basic
    e. real
    f. rand
    g. auto
    h. entry
    i. DEFAULT

20. What is the value of **string[4]** below?

```
string[20] = "abcdefghi";
```

21. Is the following expression true or false?

$$((3>2)\&\&(3<3)) \mid \mid (4==5) \mid \mid ((3>2)\&\&<3==3))$$

22. What is the meaning of the ! operator?
23. What is TRUE defined as?
24. What is FALSE defined as?
25. What is the significance of the character '\0'?
26. What is the % operator used for?
27. List the six relational operators.
28. What is the & operator?
29. Why would the variable name **milestotal** be preferable to the name **totalmiles**?
30. How is a pointer variable declared?

PROGRAMMING EXERCISES

1. Write a simple calculator program. The program will start off with a 0 for the sum and then keep one resulting number. The calculator will alternately accept operators and operands. A sample session, with comments, is listed below.

USER:	CALC	Executes Program
PROGRAM:	The current sum is 0	
	Enter a number:	
USER:	22	
PROGRAM:	The current sum is 22	
	Enter an operation:	
USER:	+	
PROGRAM:	The current sum is 22	
	Enter a number:	
USER:	39	
PROGRAM:	The current sum is 61	
	Enter an operation:	

The Program must accept integers between 1 and 32,000 inclusive as arguments and be capable of displaying results up to 47,000,000. It must process the operations listed at the top of the next page.

+	Add current result to next number
–	Subtract the next number from current result
*	Multiply current result by next number
/	Divide current result by next number
c	Clear — set the current result to 0
C	Same as c
q	Exit the program
Q	Same as q

2. Modify the simple calculator program written in Exercise 1 to accept floating point arguments and display a floating point result.

3. The following program simulates the falling of a ball from a set height with a default horizontal velocity of 1. Modify the program to use floating point variables for acceleration and height. Test the program with fractional accelerations.

```
main()

{

        /* simulate falling ball */
        int height,vel=0,damping=2;
        int acc=-1;
        height = 80;
        while(height>0 ){
          printit(height);
          height=height+vel;
          vel+=acc;
          if(height<=0){
              vel=(-damping)-vel;
              if(vel<0)vel=0;
              height=0;
              }
          }
}
printit(hgt)
int hgt;
{
    int x;
    for(x=1;x<hgt;x++)printf("x");
    printf("X\n");
}
```

4. Modify the falling object program in Exercise 3 to make the object bounce when it hits the "ground." Try the program with the velocity negated when the object hits. Then try it with the magnitude of the velocity being decreased at each bounce.

5. Write a program which will accept a command and draw the corresponding shape. The commands are:

s   small square
S   large square
c   small circle
C   large circle
r   small rectangle - full width of screen
R   large rectangle - higher rectangle than small one

Try different ASCII characters to find the best looking shapes.

BITWISE
OPERATIONS

LEARNING OBJECTIVES

- Introduce the logical AND, OR, and XOR operations.
- Demonstrate the use of C operators for performing logical operations.
- Introduce the one's complement operator.
- Introduce bit fields.

Chapter

BITWISE
OPERATIONS

5.1 OPERATING AT THE BIT LEVEL

When writing systems-level programs that deal with the hardware of the computer, it is often necessary to deal with the lowest level of data, the bit. Computer hardware usually communicates in groups of bits (usually 8, 16, or 32), where each bit may have a special meaning. In order to communicate at this level, a program must be able to deal with individual bits.

The C language includes operations for manipulating the bits within a variable. We will assume that all operations are performing on a 16-bit integer variable. Figure 5.1 shows how we represent a 16-bit integer.

15	14	13	12	11	10	9	8	7	6	5	4	3	2	1	0

FIGURE 5.1

Bit 15 is the most significant and bit 0 is the least significant. Each of these bits can be one of two states, on (1) or off (0). The value of each of the bits in the on condition is shown in the table at the top of the next page.

Value of Bits in Four Bases

	Decimal	Binary	Octal	Hex
bit 0	1	0000000000000001	000001	0001
bit 1	2	0000000000000010	000002	0002
bit 2	4	0000000000000100	000004	0004
bit 3	8	0000000000001000	000010	0008
bit 4	16	0000000000010000	000020	0010
bit 5	32	0000000000100000	000040	0020
bit 6	64	0000000001000000	000100	0040
bit 7	128	0000000010000000	000200	0080
bit 8	256	0000000100000000	000400	0100
bit 9	512	0000001000000000	001000	0200
bit 10	1024	0000010000000000	002000	0400
bit 11	2048	0000100000000000	004000	0800
bit 12	4096	0001000000000000	010000	1000
bit 13	8192	0010000000000000	020000	2000
bit 14	16384	0100000000000000	040000	4000
bit 15	32768	1000000000000000	100000	8000

FIGURE 5.2

Hexadecimal and octal are the most common ways of representing binary data. An octal digit represents three bits. The value of these bits are added to result in a number from 0 to 7.

Bit Pattern	Octal Value	Value of 16-bit word
000	0	
001	1	1 111 111 111 111 111
010	2	
011	3	1 7 7 7 7 7
100	4	
101	5	177777
110	6	
111	7	

FIGURE 5.3

A hexadecimal, or simply hex, digit represents four bits. Since the maximum value of a 4-bit number is 15, hexadecimal requires the use of the letters A – F to represent the four bits.

Bit Pattern	Hex Value	Value of 16-bit word
0000	0	
0001	1	1111 1111 1111 1111
0010	2	
0011	3	F F F F
0100	4	
0101	5	FFFF
0110	6	
0111	7	
1000	8	
1001	9	
1010	A	
1011	B	
1100	C	
1101	D	
1110	E	
1111	F	

FIGURE 5.4

The total of all 16 bits is 65,535 or 2 to the 16th power minus 1.

decimal	bit pattern	octal	hex
65535	1111111111111111	177777	FFFF

In C, octal constants are represented by beginning the constant with a '0' (number 0), and hex constants begin with a '0x'. For example, 255 decimal equals 0177 and also equals 0x7F.

5.2 SIGNED INTEGERS

When dealing with signed integers, the left-most bit is the sign bit. Therefore, the largest positive integer that can be represented in a 16-bit word is 32,767. This is the sign bit off and all other bits on.

32767 = 0x7fff = 077777 = 0111111111111111b

To represent a negative number we subtract the number from zero and borrow from an imaginary 17th bit (on many machines this is not imaginary, but is actually a flag which signifies that a negative number was produced by the operation). To represent the number −1 as a 16-bit signed integer we turn all of the bits on.

−1 = 0xffff = 0177777 = 1111111111111111b

The largest negative number we can produce this way is −32,768.

−32768 = 0x8000 = 0100000 = 1000000000000000b

These basic rules also apply to larger or smaller signed integers.

5.3 BITWISE OPERATORS

The bitwise operators perform the Boolean functions commonly used by assembly language programmers. These operators can be used on integer, including long, and character variables and constants. If you are not familiar with Boolean operations, read this section carefully. If you are already an accomplished assembly language programmer, just look at the table at the end of the chapter.

There are three basic Boolean operations to consider, the **OR**, the **AND**, and the **XOR** (exclusive or). These are all operations which require two arguments. The C operators for these three operations are:

```
&       AND
|       OR
^       XOR
```

For instance, the following expression:

result = arg1 & arg2

will set the variable **result** to the logical **AND** of **arg1** and **arg2**. The **AND** will be performed on a bit by bit basis. The results of each of the bitwise operations can be determined by looking at the following table. To use this table, find the value of the first argument along the top, the second argument down the left side, and the result is the corresponding box (shown at the top of the next page).

	AND	
	0	1
0	0	0
1	0	1

FIGURE 5.5

This shows that the only time a 1 can result with the **AND** function is when the first argument **AND** the second are both 1. When anything is **AND**ed with 0, the result is 0. The **AND** is commonly used in masking operations. Masking is a means of removing part of a variable. For example:

```
      1010101010101010     0xAAAA     0125252
  &
      0000000011111111     0x00FF     0000377
      _____
      0000000010101010     0x00AA     0000252
```

Masking is performed when a part of a variable is needed, but the remainder need not be considered. The code

    char choice;
    .
    .
    .
    choice = choice & 0x7F;

will mask off everything but the right-most seven bits of a character. This procedure can be used to normalize a character when it is not known whether the hardware supplying the character is setting bit 7. The sequence:

    a = 0x55
    b = 0x0f
    x = a & b

will put the lower four bits of **a** into **x**. The final value of **x** is 0x05.

The ¦ operator performs a bitwise logical **OR** operation on two arguments. The OR operation sets a bit to 1 if either of the corresponding bits is set in the arguments.

	OR	
	0	1
0	0	1
1	1	1

FIGURE 5.6

The sequence:

```
char choice
       .
       .
choice = getchar();
if(choice >='A' && choice <= 'Z')choice = choice | 0x20;
```

will set bit 5 on any uppercase characters entered into the program. Setting bit 5 changes uppercase characters to lowercase. The **OR** operation is often used to turn on bits within a variable. This is the quickest way to set a hardware switch. For example:

	1010101010101010	0xAAAA	0125252
|	0000000011111111	0x00FF	0000377
	1010101011111111	0xAAFF	0125377

Notice that the **&&** conditional operator in the code segment above is different from **&**, the bitwise **AND** operator.

The ^ operator performs a bitwise logical XOR, or exclusive or, operation on two arguments. The XOR will result in a one if either of the arguments is one, but not when both of the arguments are one.

	XOR	
	0	1
0	0	1
1	1	0

FIGURE 5.7

For example:

```
a = 'A'
b = 'b'
x = a ^ 0x20      /*XOR case bit */
y = b ^ 0x20      /*XOR case bit */
```

will set the sixth bit from the right to 1 if it was previously 0, and to 0 if it was previously 1. Since the letter A has an ASCII value of 0x21 the result will be 0x61 which corresponds to the ASCII character a. The letter b has an ASCII value of 0x62 so the exclusive OR will clear the sixth bit, giving a result of 0x22, which corresponds to the ASCII value for the letter B.

The best way to understand an exclusive OR operation is to remember that if the bits in the arguments are equal then the result will be a 0; otherwise, the result will be a 1. *true if different*

5.4 UNARY BIT MANIPULATION

In addition to the Boolean operators which operate on two arguments, there are bitwise operators which operate on a single variable. The two shift operators, $>>$ and $<<$, both move the bits within a variable. When bits are shifted off the end, they are lost forever. The spaces created on the other end of the variable are filled with 0. The operation:

```
x = 0x11 << 1
```

will result in a value of 0x22. The operation:

```
x = 0x11 >> 1
```

will result in 0x08. The $>>$ and $<<$ are the only operations in which knowing the word size is important. If multiple shifts are being performed, you must be aware that bits may be shifted left off the end and lost. These operations are often combined with masking operations to insure that only the bits that are of interest are operated upon. The behavior of the right shift operator is machine dependent when the sign bit is set to 1. (This is true for negative numbers.) Some machines will fill the left of the word with the sign bit, while others will fill with 0.

The last bitwise operator is the 1's complement, or unary minus operator, ~. Its operation is very simple. It reverses the value of all the bits in its argument. Therefore:

```
x = ~0x000F
```

will set **x** to 0xFFF0, assuming **x** is a 16-bit quantity. If it is longer, all the left bits will be set and only the right-most four will be cleared. This is one way of building negative masks when you are not sure of the word lengths you are dealing with. The following clears the lower four bits of an integer:

```
result = number & ~0x0F
```

This will yield 0xFFF0 if you are dealing with 16-bit quantities and 0xFFFFFFF0 if you are dealing with 32-bit quantities.

5.5 BIT FIELDS

The C language allows the definition of bit-level variables within a structure. Structures are discussed later in the book, but we will briefly discuss their use with bit fields. The following example defines a structure type called **header** and declares a variable **firstchar** of that type. The structure defines a byte which contains 4 flags and a 3-bit counter.

```
struct header{
        unsigned command : 1;    /* command/data flag */
        unsigned capture : 1;    /* save this data if flag set */
        unsigned status  : 1;    /* status request only - no data */
        unsigned correct : 1;    /* type of error correction in data */
        unsigned repeat  : 3;    /* repeat count up to 8 times */
} firstchar;
```

To test the value of these flags we address the individual items within the structure (**structure name.field** addresses a part of the structure).

```
if(firstchar.command == 1)execute();
if(firstchar.capture == 1)capture();
```

Each field within the structure must be completely contained within an integer boundary. Memory will be allocated only in increments of integer-sized bytes (on a 16-bit machine with 16-bit integers, this means a word at a time). Some of the properties of bit fields are compiler and machine dependent, so write and run a test program before embarking on a development project. A simple test program is included in the examples at the end of the chapter.

5.6 SUMMARY OF BIT OPERATIONS

The C language provide operators for manipulating integer and character variables at the bit level. These operators are listed below.

&	Performs AND operation
¦	Performs OR operation
^	Performs exclusive OR operation (XOR)
<<	Left shifts number of bits
>>	Right shifts number of bits
~	Uses the one's complement of the argument

In addition, C allows the definition of bit-level variables within a structure using the bit field data type. This creates a clean way of addressing single or multiple bits within a structure.

REVIEW QUESTIONS

1. What are the decimal values of the following constants?
   a. 023
   b. 077
   c. 0x34
   d. 010000
   e. 0x10000
   f. 03007
   g. 0xFFFF
   h. 077777
2. What is the value of bit 14?
3. How many bits are required to store the number 74,234?
4. What is the value of bit 15?

5. What are the results of the following calculations?
   a. 0x55 & 0x33
   b. 0x55 ¦ 0x33
   c. 170 & 0x77
   d. 033 + 05
   e. 'A' ^ 0x20
   f. 'a' ^ 040
   g. (0x07 < < 1) & 0x0D
   h. 0x01 < < 7
   i. (0x33 < < 4) > > 4
6. What is the C symbol for the AND operator?
7. What is the C symbol for the OR operator?
8. What is the C symbol for the XOR operator?
9. Upon which data types can Boolean operations be performed?
10. What is the difference between **&&** and **&**?
11. What is the ~ operator?
12. What is the effect of shifting an integer left one bit?
13. How many meaningful bits are there in a type char?
14. Convert the following binary numbers to decimal, octal, and hex. Assume the numbers are unsigned.
    a. 000000000000001
    b. 000000000001111
    c. 010000000000000
    d. 111111111111111
    e. 1001100110011001
    f. 0001001000110100
15. Which bit is the sign bit in a 16-bit integer?
16. What is the largest value of an unsigned 16-bit integer.
17. How is a negative number represented in a signed integer?
18. What is the bit pattern for a 16-bit integer with the value of −1?
19. If the result of the following operation

    number & 1

    is nonzero, what do you know about the value of the variable **number**?
20. What does the operation

    number ¦ = 1;

    do to the variable **number**?

21. What operation can be used to perform the converse of the operation in question 14?
22. How many bits are in an integer variable?
23. How many bits are in a char variable?
24. What is the decimal value of an integer with all bits on? (Be careful).
25. Do bit fields increase memory requirements in a program?
26. How large can any element of a bit field be?
27. How will memory be allocated in bit fields?
28. Which of the following statements contain errors?
    a. x = 23 ¦ 35
    b. y = 11.6 & 34
    c. z = 7257823 & 123777
    d. x = y & 0x1f
    e. x = y & 3ff
29. Which of the following statements contain errors?
    a. x & = 0x3f
    b. y < = 3
    c. x ˆ = 0xf0
    d. x ˜ = 0x0a
    e. x ¦¦ = 0x20
30. What is the case bit in ASCII?

PROGRAMMING EXERCISES

1. Modify the following program to change all lowercase characters in the file being copied to uppercase before writing them out to the destination file. Do not change the value of nonalphabetic characters.

```
/* A quick copy program with no error checking */
#include <stdio.h>    /* stdio.h contains equates for file I/O */
main()
{
    char ch;
    FILE *source;
    FILE *destination;
    char srcename[20];
    char destname[20];

    printf("\nEnter the source file name. ");
    scanf("%s",srcename);
```

continued

```
printf("\nEnter the destination file name. ");
scanf("%s",destname);
source=fopen(srcename,"r");
destination=fopen(destname,"w");

while((ch=fgetc(source)) != EOF)fputc(ch,destination);
exit();
}
```

2. Write a program to copy a file and mask off the high-order bit of each character. This is sometimes necessary when moving files from a system where bit 7 is always on with ASCII characters, to systems where it is off.
3. Write a function to count the number of bits that are "on" in an integer.
4. The following incomplete function should pack an array of characters into integer variables. The characters are packed two per integer. Complete the function by adding the code that does the packing.

```
main();
{
char s1[]='abcdefghijklmnop'
int array1[20];
int length;
int i;
length=packchar(s1,array);
for(i=0;i<length;i++){
        printf("Value of int %d = %d.\n"i,array[i]);
        }
}

int packchar(string,array)
char string[];
int array[];
{
int index1 = 0;
int index2 = 0;

while(string[index1] != '0'){
  /*       add the rest of the function here */


return(index2);
```

5. Write a function to unpack the array created in Example 4.
6. Write a program which will print the bit pattern of a number entered from the keyboard. The output should look like this:

120 decimal = 000000001111000 binary

7. Write a number-pattern guess program. The program should tell you if the integer you enter has the right number of bits set, too many bits, or too few. How many tries should you need to guess the number once the correct number of bits is found? The program can be limited to numbers between 0 and 255.

8. Write a program to determine what portion of an integer is used. For example, if the number 15 is entered, the program should respond that only the lower 4 bits are used. If the number 20,000 is entered, it should respond that 15 bits are used.

9. Write a program to perform the function described in Exercise 8 and then reverse the bits within the used portion. For example, entering the number 10 (1010) will yield the result 5(0101), entering the number 48(110000) will yield the number 3(000011).

10. The following program demonstrates bit fields. Enter and execute it on your system.

```
/*
    A small demo of bit manipulation

/
main()
{
    struct byte{
        unsigned bit0 : 1;
        unsigned bit1 : 1;
        unsigned rest : 6;
        }onebyte;
    int pad = 0;    /* This is here so we can print onebyte as
                        an integer to show its value in hex. */
    char ch;

    printf("\nPress a key  ");
    ch = getchar();
    assign(&onebyte,&ch);   /* use pointers to move value to onebyte */
    printf("\nThe character %c = %x hex.\n",onebyte,onebyte);
    if(onebyte.bit0 == 1)printf("The first defined bit is on.\n");
    if(onebyte.bit1 == 1)printf("The second defined bit is on.\n");
    printf("The value of variable rest is %x hex.\n",onebyte.rest);
    printf("\n Goodbye \n");
    }
/*
    This function is used to assign mismatched data types.  It will
    indiscriminately write over data if the pointer definition here
    is for a data type longer than the destination variable.  Use
    with extreme caution.
*/
assign(p1,p2)
char *p1,*p2;
{
    *p1=*p2;
    }
```

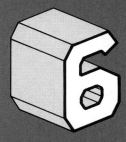

CONTROL FLOW
AND LOOPS

LEARNING OBJECTIVES

- Introduce the **if-else** statement.
- Describe **switch** and **case** statements.
- Describe basic loop types and structure.
- Cover **while**, **for**, and **do-while** loops.
- Describe the **break** and **continue** statements.
- Discuss the use of labels and the **goto** statement.

Chapter

CONTROL FLOW AND LOOPS

6.1 CONTROL FLOW IN A C PROGRAM

The control flow of a program is the sequence in which instructions are executed. Without being told otherwise, C programs will follow the simplest path, beginning execution at the first line of executable code in function **main**, and going until execution falls off the end of the program. That is the simplest control flow. Luckily, the control flow can be modified by conditional statements, loops, and the **goto** statement (which we generally avoid trying to use). The statements will look familiar, since we have been using them in our examples since the beginning of the book. The basic types of control statements in C are described as follows:

The **if-else** pair allows conditional execution of a group of statements.

The **switch-case** allows the conditional execution of one of a number of groups of statements based on the value of a variable.

The **while** is a loop construct which allows for the repeated execution of a group of statements as long as a condition is true. The condition is checked each time before the code is executed.

The **for** loop is a specialized type of **while** loop. It includes an initialization statement which is executed once before the condition is checked and an expression which is executed at the end of the loop before control is transferred back to the test at the loop's beginning.

The **do-while** loop is like the **while**, except that the condition is checked after the loop is executed.

The **break** statement terminates execution of a loop or **switch-case** and transfers execution to the first statement following the loop.

The **continue** statement causes execution to pass to the end of the current loop.

The **goto** statement transfers control to a location specified by a label.

Each of the control structures has special properties which make it suitable for certain situations. The trick is to decide when to use each type of structure.

6.2 IF-ELSE STATEMENTS

The format of the **if-else** is simple and logical. The **else** portion of the statement is optional. The basic format is:

```
if (expression)
    statement;

else
    statement;
```

or without the **else**, it is simply:

```
if (expression)
    statement;
```

The statement can either be a simple statement terminated by a **;** or a compound statement enclosed in braces ({ }). For example, the two following **if** statements are equivalent

```
if(x == y) return(0);
if(x == y){
    return(0);
    }
```

In both of these statements the **return(0)** will be executed if **x** is equal to **y**. The expression inside the **if** test can be anything that has a value. For example:

```
a = x==y;
if(a)return(0);
```

is equivalent to

```
if(x == y) return(0);
```

because the logical value of **x = = y** has been assigned to the variable **a**. Variable **a** is then equal to 0 (false) or 1 (true).

Each **if** can have one and only one **else** associated with it. The statement after the else is executed if the expression within the **if** is false. For example:

```
if(x == y)
      return(0);
else
      return(1);
```

will return the value of 1 if **x** does not equal **y**. Of course the same thing could be accomplished by:

```
return(x!=y);
```

which would return true (1) if **x** does not equal **y**, and 0 otherwise.

The statements after **if** and **else** can also be statement groups as in

```
if(x == y){
      printf("Illegal values passed to this routine.\n");
      return(-1);
      }
else{
      z = temp1/(x-y);
      return(z);
      }
```

The **else** always belongs to the **if** immediately preceding it. This is a point which must be carefully watched when there are multiple or nested **if** statements. In the code

```
if(x == y)
     if(n > 10)
          printf("The proper conditions have been met.\n");
else
     printf("x does not equal y");
```

the indenting implies that the **else** goes with the **if(x == y)**, but the compiler will place it with the last **if** which is **if(n > 10)**. This type of error can produce the type of bug that can prove difficult to find, since the program looks like it absolutely has to work. The easiest way to avoid this sort of problem is always to use braces with **if** statements. So the example above becomes

```
if(x == y){
    if(n > 10){
        printf("The proper conditions have been met.\n");
    }
}
else{
    printf("x does not equal y");
}
```

Some of these braces are unnecessary, but they cost nothing and they make the program easier to read.

Another common form taken by the **if-else** statement takes place when multiple **if** comparisons are chained. This leads to the construct **else-if**. For example, the program launch program in Chapter 3 could be expanded to check for multiple languages and to run multiple programs. This example accepts four languages.

```
/* Another very short demo program.  This program checks
   a launch code and exits if it is incorrect.  If a
   correct code is entered the appropriate function is
   called. */
main()
{
    char lnchcode[10];
    printf("Enter your launch code");
    getcode(lnchcode);
    if(strcmp(lnchcode,"ALGOL") == 0)oldfashioned()
    else if(strcmp(lnchcode,"COBOL") == 0)wordy();
    else if(strcmp(lnchcode,"APL") == 0)greektome();
    else if(strcmp(lnchcode,"FORTH")==0)stackedwrong();
    else{
        printf("Your launch code is incorrect.\n");
        printf("Please contact your instructor.\n");
        errorexit();
    }
    exit();
}
```

FIGURE 6.1

This program is not complete, but it serves to illustrate the use of the **else-if** construct. The program makes use of the system function **strcmp** to compare the user's string with the various keywords. The function **strcmp** returns a value *false?* of zero when the two strings being compared are equal.

Using the **else-if** in the number guess program saves the work of one compare.

```
/*
Number Guess Program with else-if statements

*/
#define MAXNUM 10
main()

{
/* This program creates a number between 1 and 10.   It
   then accepts the user's guesses and gives hints  */

int number,guess;

printf("\nThis program will select a number from 1 to 10.\n");
printf("Try to guess the number in the fewest tries.");

number=getran(MAXNUM);
while((guess = getnum(MAXNUM)) != 99){

    if(guess > number){
        printf("Your guess was too high.\n");
        }
    else if(guess < number){
        printf("Your guess was too low.\n");
        }
    else{
        reward();
        number=grtran(MAXNUM);
        break;
        }

    }
printf("Thank you for using this program.\n");
}    /* end of main program */
```

FIGURE 6.2

By reversing the order of the checks and nesting the **if** statements, we have made the right answer a fall-through rather than an explicitly checked-for case.

It is traditional to write the **else-if** as we have in these two programs even though proper indenting of a program with three **if**s would look more like this:

```
if (expression)
    statement1;
else
    if(expression)
        statement2;
    else
        if(expression)
            statement3;
```

The problem with multiple levels of indentation is that they produce increasingly deep levels of indentation until the code cascades off the right-hand edge of the screen — without increasing readability.

6.3 SWITCH AND CASE

The **switch-case** pair is an alternative to nested or repeated **if**s in some cases. Take, for example, the case of a program that inputs a menu choice, as in this segment of code from a test bank generator program.

```
mainmenu();
x=getkey(&choice);
switch(choice){
      case 'a':
      case 'A':
            designtst();
            endflg=0;
            break;
      case 'b':
      case 'B':
            loadtst();
            endflg=0;
            break;
      case 'c':
      case 'C':
            reviewchp();
            break;
      case 'd':
      case 'D':
            editchp();
            break;
```

FIGURE 6.3 *(Part 1 of 2)*

```
        case 'e':
        case 'E':
              edithdr(1);
              break;
        case hlpkey:
              help1();
              break;
        case 27:  /* 27 is the Esc key */
              endflg=1;
              break;
        default:
              beep();
              break;
        }       /* end of main menu switch */
```

FIGURE 6.3 *(Part 2 of 2)*

Notice that each **case** statement is terminated by a colon. The colon is used in C to create labels that mark program locations. A series of **cases** are really just markers within the block of code contained in the **switch**. Control is transferred to the first **case** that matches the result of the expression in the **switch** statement.

The format of the **switch** statement is:

```
switch(expression){
      case constant1:
            statement1;
            break;
      case constant2:
            statement2;
            break;
      default:
            statement3;
            break;
      }
```

The expression here must produce an integer or character result, and each of the constants must be an integer or a character. When this code is executed, the expression in the **switch** statement is evaluated and compared to each of the **case** constants in order. If a match is found, execution is started at that **case** statement. If no match is found, control is transferred to the **default** statement.

The **break** statement causes an immediate exit from the **switch**. This is necessary, since the **switch** merely passes control to the code contained in the proper **case**. Without the **break** statement, processing will continue and any **case** code that follows will also be executed. We will cover **break** completely a little later in the chapter.

6.4 LOOPS

There are two basic types of loops:

1. **The Unconditional loop** — This is the type of loop that was generally implemented with a **goto** before the advent of structured programming. The use of **goto**s is now considered bad taste, so unconditional loops are now usually implemented with a conditional loop where the condition is always true.
2. **The Conditional loop** — This is the more common of the two basic loop types. This is a loop where there is a built-in **if** condition. The code within the loop gets executed **if** the condition is true.

We will concentrate our discussion on the conditional loop constructs available in C.

There are two types of conditional loops. The first one checks the condition at the beginning of the code to be executed. This works out to, "If this condition is true, execute the following code." At the end of the code sequence, control is returned back to the beginning of the loop and the condition is checked again. In C, this type of loop is implemented with the **while** and the **for** constructs. For example:

```
/* Print an interesting series of numbers */
main()
{
int sum;
sum = 1;
while(sum < 100){
    sum = sum+sum;
    printf("sum = %d\n",sum);
    }
}
```

FIGURE 6.4

This loop will be executed as long as the variable **sum** is less than 100. If the initial value of **sum** had been greater than 100, the code within the loop would not have been executed. The output from this program will be:

```
sum = 2
sum = 4
sum = 8
sum = 16
sum = 32
sum = 64
sum = 128
```

FIGURE 6.5

Notice that one number greater than 100 is printed. This is because the variable **sum** was less than 100 on the last iteration when the test was performed at the top of the loop. When designing loops, pay special attention to the end conditions: The first and last pass through the loop cause the most problems with loops.

The second type of conditional loop has the check at the end of the code. Thus the code is always executed once, and is then executed again each time **if** the condition is true. In C this type is implemented with the **do-while** construct.

```
do {
    code in here
    }
while(condition);
```

Let's examine each of the loop constructs in detail.

6.5 WHILE LOOPS

The most basic loop structure offered in C is the **while** loop. The syntax is straightforward.

```
while(expression)
    statement;
```

The statement or group of statements "inside" the **while** loop will be executed repeatedly until the expression is false.

The following program will print an approximation to the series:

$$e = 1 + 1/1! + 1/2! 1/3! + 1/4! + 1/5! + 1/6! + 1/7! \ldots$$
where $5! = 5*4*3*2*1.$

This is the series used to calculate **e**, the base of natural logarithms. It is also a simple series to calculate on a computer. This program approximates **e** to 10 decimal places.

```
/* Calculate the value of e using a while loop */

#define LIMIT 1.0e-10
main()
{
    double counter = 1.0;
    double fraction = 1.0;
    double denom = 1.0;
    double total = 0.0;
    while(fraction > LIMIT){
        fraction = 1.0/denom;
        denom *=counter;
        counter++;
        total += fraction;
        }
    printf("Limit = %1.10f after %f iterations.\n", total, counter);
    }
```

FIGURE 6.6

This program will add progressively smaller increments to the total until the amount being added is less than the constant, **LIMIT**.

The **while** loop may contain only a simple statement as in

```
while(account != userno)account = getaccount();
```

where the program will continue to perform the statement

```
account = getaccount();
```

until **account** is equal to **userno**.

The expressions within the **while** loop condition often contain calculations and function calls. For example, the line of code below skips to the end of a line of text that is being read from file **fp**.

```
while((ch=fgetc(fp)) != '\n'){};
```

The conditional expression contains the work done by this **while** loop, the statement performed as long as the condition is true is the null statement {}. The next line of code can then start reading from the next line of the file.

6.6 THE FOR LOOP

One sequence of code commonly seen in programs is:

```
/* initialize the array x */
i=0;
while(i<100){
     x[i]=i;
     i++;
     }
```

This sequence initializes an array by setting each element to its index. The four components of this sequence are the initialization assignment (**i = 0**), the conditional loop statement (**while(i < 100)**), the code that initializes the array (**x[i] = i**), and the assignment which modifies the loop variable (**i + +**).

In the C language this can be expressed more concisely using a **for** loop

```
for(i=0;i<100;i++)x[i]=i;
```

The **for** loop is a general purpose construct, but it is most commonly used in loops where there are one or more indices to manage. The format of the **for** statement is:

```
for(expression;expression;expression)statement;
```

where all three expressions are optional. The expressions can be any legal expression, but they generally match three of the components of the **while** loop in the example at the beginning of this section.

The first component is the initialization expression. This expression will be executed at the beginning of the loop upon entry. The second component is the condition. This is the relational expression that would be placed in the equivalent **while** loop. The last component is a statement to be performed at the end of the loop before checking the condition to see if another iteration is to be performed.

The simplest **for** loop is the one containing no expressions

for(;;)statement;

This is an infinite loop where the statement will be executed until the loop is interrupted. This is a useful construct for cases where you wish to loop forever. For example, see Figure 6.7.

```
/* a simple adding machine which runs an infinite total */
main()
{
int number;
int total;
total = 0;
printf("\n\nThis program will total a string of numbers.\n");
printf("Type in the numbers one at a time, and the program ");
printf("will print\na running total.  Press ctrl C to ");
printf("terminate the program.\n\n");

for(;;){
    printf("\nThe current total is %d. \n\n",total);
    printf("Enter the next number. ");
    scanf("%d",&number);     /* get the next number  */
    total += number;
    }
}
```

FIGURE 6.7

In this program the **for** loop just keeps the print-getnumber-calculate sequence going forever. As an interesting experiment, try using this program to calculate large sums. What happens when the total exceeds a 15-bit amount (or 31 bits if an **int** is 32 bits on your machine)? What happens when it exceeds a 16-bit sum?

The example, at the top of the next page, shows a typical application of **for** loops. This function deletes a number of characters from the middle of a string. The **for** statements are used to manage the indices as the string is compressed.

```
/* strngdel  - delete characters from a string
   call with - starting position of substring to delete (int)
             - Number of characters to delete (int)
             - Pointer to the string (pointer - see next chapter)
*/
strngdel(startpos,nchars,string)
int startpos;                       /* position to start delete */
int nchars;                         /* number of positions to delete */
char string[];                      /* pointer to string */
{
     int length;                    /* length of string - calculated */
     int j;
     /* find the length of the string */
     for(length = 0;string[length] != '\0' ; ++length);
     if(startpos > length)
          return(-1);              /* starting char beyond end of string */
     for(j = startpos; j < length; j++){
          string[j] = string[j + nchars];
     }
     return(nchars);
}
```

FIGURE 6.8

The real strength of the **for** loop becomes obvious when there are nested loops. Take the routine below as an example. This routine searches a three-dimensional array for all occurrences of a certain value.

```
/* scan an array searching for target */
int array[10][10][10];
int i,j,k,hits;
int target;



hits = 0;
for(i=0;i<10;i++){
     for(j=0;j<10;j++){
          for(k=0;k<10;k++){
               if(array[i][j][k] == target)hits++;
               }
          }
     }
```

FIGURE 6.9

This simple set of loops would be much more complicated if it were implemented using **while** loops.

```
int array[10][10][10];
int i,j,k,hits;
hits = 0;



i=0;
while(i<10){
     j=0;
     while(j<10){
          k=0;
          while(k<10){
               if(array[i][j][k] == target)hits++;
               k++;
               }
          j++
          }
     i++;
     }
```

FIGURE 6.10

As you can see, using the **for** statement makes the loop structure simpler and cleaner.

The **for** loop is also commonly used for processing and producing lists and tables. The program in Figure 6.11 creates the list of ASCII values and the C language representation. You will notice that there is special code to handle different cases. Running this will produce the file **TEXT** which will contain the table. The only problem that you will have is that not all the characters are printable, so that the file will have to be examined using the text editor to see all displayable characters.

The program in Figure 6.11 will produce a table of 128 numbers in decimal, octal, and hex with the proper representation of that ASCII character in C. It does not show the special C representation for tabs, end of line, and backspace characters. These were added to the table manually for the appendix.

```
/*
    Print a table of decimal, octal, and hex numbers with
    the ASCII equivalent and the C code.
*/

#include <stdio.h>
main()
{
    FILE *fp;
    char s[9]="        ";
    char s2[5];
    int let=0;
    fp=fopen("TEXT","w");
    fprint(fp,"\n        Decimal    Octal    Hex     c code\n\n");
    for(let = 0 ; let < 129;let++){
        if(let >32){
            s2{0}=let;
            s2{1}='\0';
            }
        else{
            s2{0}='\\';
            sprintf(&s2{1},"%d\0",let);
            }
        fprintf(fp,"%s%3d%s%3o%s%2x%s%s%\n"
            ,"     ",let,s,let,s,let,s,s2);
    }
}
```

FIGURE 6.11

Decimal	Octal	Hex	C code
0	0	0	\0
1	1	1	\1
2	2	2	\2
.			
.			
.			
31	37	1F	\31
32	40	20	\32
33	41	21	!
34	42	22	"
35	43	23	#
.			
.			
.			

FIGURE 6.12 *(Part 1 of 2)*

Decimal	Octal	Hex	C code
118	166	76	v
119	167	77	w
120	170	78	x
121	171	79	y
122	172	7A	z
123	173	7B	{
124	174	7C	|
125	175	7D	}
126	176	7E	~
127	177	7F	?
128	200	80	

FIGURE 6.12 *(Part 2 of 2)*

This table will be printed with the empty spaces filled in, of course.

Since the expressions in a **for** loop can be anything, the compiler does not treat loop index variables in any special manner. There is no rule against modifying a loop variable inside a loop. This is definitely a mixed blessing, however. Take for example this line of code which is supposed to delete a character in a string by rolling back all characters following it by one.

```
string[27] = "ABCDEFGHIJKLMNOPQRSTUVWXYZ"
dchar=10;
for(i=dchar;i<length;i++)string[i]=string[++i];
```

When printed, the resulting string will look something like:

```
ABCDEFGHIJLLNNPPRRTTVVXXZZ
```

with some sort of garbage following it (you get the garbage because the program wrote over the \0, which terminates the string).

The problem is obvious in this case. The loop index, **i**, is being modified in two places.

```
string[27] = "ABCDEFGHIJKLMNOPQRSTUVWXYZ"
dchar=10;
for(i=dchar;i<length;  i++  )string[i]=string[  ++i  ];
```

The problems resulting from this sort of mistake are not always obvious. When the symptoms are not obviously caused by an index problem, the mistake can be very difficult to find, especially when the code inside the loop is long and complex. The best policy is to avoid modifying loop variables.

6.7 DO-WHILE LOOPS

The **do-while** construct is not as commonly used as the **while** and the **for** loops. The **do-while** allows the programmer to design a loop with the check performed after the code inside the loop executes. The format is

do statement;
while(expression);

The main reason for using **do-while** is the need for the code inside the loop to be executed at least once. For example:

```
main()
{
      .
      .
      .
do{
      dspmenu();
      choice = getchoice();
      doaction(choice);
      }
while(choice != QUIT);
}
```

FIGURE 6.13

This program displays the menu, gets the users choice, and does whatever the user asks as long as the user does not choose the quit option. The reason for choosing the **do-while** construct is that the program must perform the code at least once. Of course, the same loop could be implemented with a plain **while** as long as the initial value of the variable **choice** was not equal to **QUIT**.

Note that the **do-while** condition test is the opposite of that in the Pascal **Repeat-until** loop. When translating programs from Pascal to C this fact can be easily overlooked, so be careful.

6.8 BREAK

Loops are usually executed as long as the condition contained in the **while** or **for** expression is valid. The **break** statement provides an alternate way of getting out of a loop. A **break** statement is usually associated with an **if** statement inside a loop. This combination allows the programmer to handle the special case where an early exit from the loop is desirable. The main reason for using a **break** is to make the main loop statement more readable. Any condition that can force a break can be contained in the conditional expression of the loop structure. For example, the following loop can be very difficult to read.

```
for(i=1;
    buf[i] != '\n' && buf[i] != '\0' && buf[i] != '\027'
    && i<maxchar;i++)string[i] = buf[i];
```

but it is more easily deciphered when written

```
for(i=0;i<maxchar;i++)[
    if(buf[i] != '\n' && buf[i] != '\0' && buf[i] != '\027')
        break;      /* get out if special char */
    string[i]=buf[i];
    ]
```

This form makes it very clear that you are copying **x** characters from array **buf** to array **string**, and that you want to stop if any of those special characters are encountered.

The other common use for the **break** statement is with the **case** statements. The **break** is used there to stop execution from "falling through" into the next **case**. Look at the example in the **switch-case** section at the beginning of this chapter.

6.9 CONTINUE

The **continue** statement provides a way to skip the rest of the code in a loop and proceed directly to the end of the loop. There is no time when you have to use a **continue** statement, but it sometimes makes code more readable while saving execution time. For example:

```
for(i=1;i<100;i++){
    if(i=x)continue;
        .
        .
        .

    }
```

is equivalent to

```
for(i=1;i<100;i++){
     if(i != x){
              .

              .
              .
     }
}
```

The use of the **continue** in the first example saves a level of indentation, but is not necessary. Using a **continue** can cause some confusion if it is not used with care, since it is equivalent to a **goto** jumping over a section of code.

6.10 LABELS AND THE GOTO STATEMENT

The **goto** statement is commonly considered a sign of bad programming. This is largely due to its justified reputation for making programs confusing and unreadable. In general **goto**s are not needed in modern programming languages. If it appears that a **goto** is required to make your program work, reexamine the program's design. The most common reason for using the **goto** is poor design.

There are times when it is just too complicated to code your way out of deeply nested loops, or when adding the code to allow an error exit causes too much overhead. For those cases, and less justifiable ones, C offers the **goto** statement and the ability to insert labels into the program. For example:

```
int array[10][10][10];
int i,j,k,hits;
hits = 0;


for(i=0;i<10;i++){
     for(j=0;j<10;j++){
          for(k=0;k<10;k++){
               if(array[i][j][k+1] == 0)goto error;
               if(array[i][j][k] == target)hits++;
               }
          }
     }
Printf("There are %d occurrences of %d in the array.\n",hits,target);
exit();
error:
printf("Error encountered by function QND.\n");
exit();
```

FIGURE 6.14

Although this looks like a reasonable application of a **goto**, it should be noted that the **goto** can always be avoided. In this case placing the error exit code inside the loop accomplishes the same thing as the **goto**. This change yields a smaller and clearer program:

```
int array[10][10][10];
int i,j,k,hits;
hits = 0;


for(i=0;i<10;i++){
    for(j=0;j<10;j++){
        for(k=0;k<10;k++){
            if(array[i][j][k+1] == 0){
                printf("Error encountered by function QND.\n");
                exit();
                ]
            if(array[i][j][k] == target)hits++;
            }
        }
    }
Printf("There are %d occurrences of %d in the array.\n",hits,target);
exit();
```

FIGURE 6.15

6.11 SUMMARY

The ability of statements to change the sequence of program execution is essential to writing useful programs. Execution order is modified by using conditional execution, loop constructs, and **goto** statements.

The C language offers two conditional execution constructs, the **if-else** pair and the **switch-case** pair. The **if-else** pair has the syntax

    if (expression)
        statement;
    else
        statement;

The **else** portion of the **if-else** pair is optional. The **switch-case** construct has the format:

```
switch(expression){
    case constant1:
        statement1;
        break;
    case constant2:
        statement2;
        break;
    default:
        statement3;
        break;
}
```

The expression in the **switch** statement must produce an integer or character. The **break** statements are used to terminate each **case** to stop execution from continuing into the next **case**.

There are three loop constructs in C, the **while** statement, the **for** statement, and the **do-while** statement. The syntax of the **while** statement is:

```
while(expression)statement;
```

The statement will be repeatedly executed as long as the expression is true. The **while** loop expression is usually a conditional or a function call that returns a true or false value.

The **for** loop has the syntax:

```
for(expression1;expression2;expression3)statement;
```

The first expression is executed when the statement is encountered and is used to initialize the loop. The second expression is the condition which determines if the statement will be executed. The third expression is executed after the statement and before the condition is checked for the next pass through the loop.

The **do-while** loop has the syntax:

```
do statement;
while(expression);
```

This is similar to the **while** loop, but the programmer is guaranteed that the statement will be executed at least once, since it is executed before the expression is checked.

In addition, the C language includes the **break** statement that will cause immediate exit from a loop, the **continue** statement which provides a way of skipping the rest of the code contained in the loop, and the **goto** which transfers control unconditionally. In well-designed programs, the use of these three statements should be minimized, with the exception of **break** statements with the **switch-case** construct.

REVIEW QUESTIONS

1. Which of the following statements is legal?
    a. if(a = = b)printf("Hello");
    b. if(a = = b){ printf("Hello")}
    c. if(a = = b){printf("Hello");}
    d. if(a)printf("Hello");
    e. if(a = = b)printf("hello);
        else printf("Goofbye");
    f. if(a = = b ¦ ¦ a>b)printf("Hello);
    g. if(a ¦ ¦ b)printf("Hello);
    h. if(a && b)printf("Hello");

2. Rewrite the following **if** statements so the operation being performed is clear.
    a. if(a = = b && c)printf("Hello);
    b. if(a = = b>0)printf("hello);
    c. if(a = = b¦¦a = = 0&&b = = 1)printf("Hello);
    d. if(a¦¦b = = 1)printf("Hello");

3. What will be printed in the following sequence?

    ```
    x=1;
    y=2;
    if(x==y)printf("ABC");
    else printf("DEF");
    ```

4. The following statement is legal, but it displays a common type of error. Find the error and correct it.

    ```
    if(ch='A')printf("Item A selected");
    ```

5. Are the following code segments operationally equivalent?

Segment 1:
```
if(a==b)printf("Hello);
```

Segment 2:
```
if(a==b){
    printf("Hello");
    }
```

6. How many **else** statements can be associated with an **if** statement?
7. What is wrong with the following sequence?

```
if(maximum == 0){
    minimum =0;
    }
median=(maximum-minimum)/2;
else {
    minimum = maximum/2;
    }
```

8. Why are **break** statements placed at the end of most **case** statements?
9. What is the function of the **default** when used with a **switch** statement?
10. Can **case** be used without **switch**?
11. Can more than one **case** be used for the same block of code? For example:

```
case 'A'
case 'a'
    printf("Choice is A");
    break;
```

12. What is wrong with the following sequence?

```
int x,y;

switch(x){
    case 3:
        printf("x = 3");
        break
    case y;
        printf("x = y");
        break;
    }
```

13. What will be printed in the following sequence?

```
x=3;

switch(x){
    case 1:
    case 2:
        printf("X<3\n");
    case 3:
        printf("X=3\n");
    case 4:
    case 5:
        printf("X>3\n");
    default:
        printf("X unknown\n");
    }
```

14. What type of arguments can be used with the **case** statement?
15. Can the following example be rewritten with a **case** statement? Explain.

```
int x,z;
x=getnumber()
if(x == z)functn1();
else if(x == z*2)functn2();
else if(x == z*3)functn3();
else if(x == z*4)functn4();
else error();
```

16. Which C statements are designed for conditional looping?
17. Which C loop structures check the condition before executing the statement contained inside the loop?
18. Which of the following code segments are legal?
    a. while(x<y)x++;
    b. while(x<y){
           x++;
           }
    c. while(x++ <y);
    d. while x < 3{
           x++;
           }
    e. while(x<y){x++}
    f. while(x<y){x++;}
19. Can there be a reason for having a **while** statement with a null statement?

20. What are the three components contained inside the parentheses of a **for** statement?
21. How many of the components of a **for** statement are required?
22. Which of the following statements are legal?
    a. for(i = 1,i < 12,i + +)x + = i;
    b. for(;i < 10;)i + +;
    c. for(i + +;i < 10;i + +)x + = i;
    d. for(i = getchar();i < compute(i*x);i = average(i,x))x + = i;
    e. for(i = 1;i < 10;i + +);
    f. for(i = fgetc;i! = '\n');
    g. for(;;i + +){
           process(i);
           }
23. What are the uses of the following loop?

    for(;;;){

    some code in here

        }

24. What is the major difference between the **do-while** and the **while** loops?
25. What is wrong with the following code sequence?

```
do{
     printf("Looping\n");
     x++;
     }
printf("At end of loop");
while(x<10);
```

26. What is the **break** statement used for in loops?
27. What do the **break**, **continue**, and **goto** statements have in common?
28. What is the effect of the **continue** statement in a loop?
29. What are the usual reasons for resorting to **goto** statements?
30. Can **goto** statements be avoided?

PROGRAMMING EXERCISES

1. Rewrite the following program segment using the **switch-case** structure.

```
if(c=getchar() == 'A'){
    loadfile();
    }
else{ if(c == 'B'){
    changedir();
    }
else{ if(c == 'C'){
    deletefil();
    }
else{ if(c == 'D'){
    catalog();
    }
else{ if(c == 'E'){
    format();
    }
else{ if(c = '\27'){
    exit();
    }
```

2. Enter the following program as shown. Then rewrite it using **case** statements. Compare the size of the two compiled programs.

```
else if(month == 1)  printf("January");
else if(month == 2)  printf("February");
else if(month == 3)  printf("March");
else if(month == 4)  printf("April");
else if(month == 5)  printf("May");
else if(month == 6)  printf("June");
else if(month == 7)  printf("July");
else if(month == 8)  printf("August");
else if(month == 9)  printf("September");
else if(month == 10) printf("October");
else if(month == 11) printf("November");
else if(month == 12) printf("December");
else {
        printf("Illegal month code");
        exit();
        }
```

3. The program segment in Example 1 assumes that all menu choices will be in uppercase. Change the program to accept uppercase and lowercase by adding **case**s for the lowercase characters.

4. Change the program segment in Example 1 to accept uppercase and lower-case characters by using the masking information at the end of the last chapter to convert lowercase characters to uppercase. What problems might this cause with special characters?

5. Write a function that accepts an integer argument and returns the factorial of that number. The factorial operation is written with an exclamation point (!) to represent the operation. The factorial of 6 is defined

$$6! = 6 * 5 * 4 * 3 * 2 * 1 = 720$$

The function should detect if the number to be returned is larger than a legal integer and return an error code of −1.

6. The numbers 1,2,3,5,8,13,21,34,..., where each number after the second is equal to the sum of the two numbers before it, are called fibonacci numbers. Write a program which will print the first 50 fibonacci numbers.

7. Change the initial value of the variable **sum** in the following program and run the program. Determine the formula for the series printed.

```
/* Print an interesting series of numbers */
main()
{
int sum;
sum = 1;
while(sum < 100){
    sum = sum+sum;
    printf("sum = %d\n",sum);
    }
}
```

8. Write a program to print a checkerboard of diamond shapes from 1 to 8 diamonds square. For example, a checkerboard 2 diamonds square would look like:

```
    *       *
   ***     ***
  *****   *****
   ***     ***
    *       *
    *       *
   ***     ***
  *****   *****
   ***     ***
    *       *
```

The program should ask the user for the size of the square to print.

9. Write a program to print statistics about a text file. The statistics required are:
   a. Number of characters in the file
   b. Number of lines in the file
   c. Number of empty lines in the file (white space only)
   d. Number of words in the file
   e. Distribution of sets of repetitive characters

   This program will be used to analyze the makeup of files for development of a file compression program. The output should look like:

   ```
   Analysis of file xxxxxx

   Length:  bytes xxxxx      words xxxxx     lines xxxx

   Number of blank lines   xxx      xx%

   Distribution of character repetition   singles  xxx    xx%
                                          doubles  xxx    xx%
                                          triples  xxx    xx%
                                          quads    xxx    xx%
                                          5-8      xxx    xx%
                                          >8       xxx    xx%
                                                   =====
                                                   100%
   ```

10. Write a program that will simulate a drunken sailor standing in the middle of a 100-foot-long bridge. The sailor will start walking at random. Each step can be toward either end of the bridge. How long will he stagger about before getting to one end? The program will have to use the **rand** function, which returns a random floating point number between 0 and 1, to decide which direction the sailor is to stagger. Assume the sailor takes one step a second, and print the time in hours, minutes, and seconds format.

PROGRAMMING PROJECT - THE DELI

Your local Deli has just installed an IBM PS/2, but they still use old-fashioned analog scales. The deli owner has written a detailed description of what he wants the PC to do. Here is the description of the PC's function:

   a. It should display a menu of the 40 deli items and their price per pound. To the left of each item should be the item number.
   b. The program should wait for an item number to be entered.

c. When the item number is entered, the program should ask for the weight of the item sold. The user then enters the weight in ounces.

d. The program should then print out the price ticket.

e. The program should then display the menu again and continue from Item 1.

f. Here is the list of items and their prices:

Bologna	2.29	Chicken Roll	2.29
German Bologna	2.19	Turkey Roll	2.39
Franks	1.99	Turkey Breast	3.29
Skinless Franks	1.99	Ham Salad	1.49
Salami — Hard	2.89	Cole Slaw	.89
Salami — Genoa	3.29	Potato Salad	.89
Salami — Cooked	2.49	Macaroni Salad	.89
Pepper Loaf	1.89	Fruit Salad	.99
Pickle + pimento	1.89	Tuna Salad	1.59
Olive Loaf	1.99	Crab Meat Salad	2.99
Luncheon loaf	1.89	Lobster Salad	3.29
Pepperoni	3.29	American Cheese	1.89
Domestic Ham	2.19	Provolone Cheese	1.99
Imported Ham	2.99	Domestic Swiss	2.09
Baked Ham	3.39	Imported Swiss	2.39
Virginia Ham	3.19	Parmesan Cheese	4.19
Hot Ham	3.19	Romano Cheese	4.19
Ham Loaf	1.99	Cherry Pie	1.29
Prosciutto	4.59	Apple Pie	1.29
Procitini	3.29	Cheesecake	1.99

As the analyst designing the program, you should be pleased with the detail of the owner's description. Now you must determine the rest of the details and write the program. For this demonstration you can output to the screen rather than the printer.

POINTERS
AND ARRAYS

LEARNING OBJECTIVES

- Discuss the concept and use of pointers.
- Discuss the relationship between pointers and arrays.
- Demonstrate the use of pointers.
- Introduce pointers to pointers.

Chapter

7

POINTERS
AND ARRAYS

7.1 POINTERS

The pointer data type is a powerful element of the C language. Pointers are variables which point to memory locations. In C every pointer has a data type associated with it to tell the compiler to what type of variable it points. The ability to deal with addresses in a high-level language offers solutions to many problems which otherwise could only be solved using assembly language. The use of addresses also allows for the construction of complex data structures with extreme flexibility.

The negative side of pointers is that they can be confusing to use at first. The ability to do extremely complex operations efficiently by using the properties of pointers imposes a cost in readability. These issues must be weighed when writing code, and the best balance found. The liberal use of comments when using pointers goes a long way toward resolving the problem. In any case, an understanding of pointers is necessary if you are to work with C, if only to understand code written by others.

We will start by declaring three variables, integers **y** and **z**, and a pointer to integers **ptry**. The declarations

```
int y;
int z;
int *ptry;
```

create these variables. The memory for these variables would look like Figure 7.1.

NAME	ADDRESS	CONTENTS
y	12754	0
z	12756	0
*ptry	12758	0

FIGURE 7.1

A declaration with the character ***** before the variable name creates a pointer. When a pointer is declared, three attributes are identified: its name, its type (pointer), and to what data type it points. You cannot create a pointer without identifying the data type with which it will be used.

We have created these three variables, but they are not initialized. We will initialize **y** with

```
y=6;
```

and continue from there. This leaves us with Figure 7.2.

NAME	ADDRESS	CONTENTS
y	12754	6
z	12756	0
*ptry	12758	0

FIGURE 7.2

There are two primary operators used in pointer operations. The address operator, **&**, returns the address of its argument. The statement

```
ptry = &y;
```

sets the pointer **ptry** to the address of the variable **y**.

NAME	ADDRESS	CONTENTS
y	12754	6
z	12756	0
ptry	12758	12754

FIGURE 7.3

In this case **ptry** will point to the number 6. Be sure that you understand the distinction between a pointer and to the data that it points. In this case **ptry** contains the address of a memory location. That memory location contains the number 6. You cannot set an integer to **ptry**. The statement

```
z = ptry  /*   INCORRECT  */
```

will not place the value 6 in **z**. It will set **z** to an address and generate warning messages from the compiler.

The other operator used with pointers is the indirection operator **∗**. This is the opposite of the address operator. The statement

```
z = *ptry;
```

sets the variable **z** to the *value pointed to by* **ptry**. In this case it will set **z** to the number 6. The two statements

```
ptry = &y;
z = *ptry;
```

have the same affect on **z** as

```
z=y;
```

These two operators provide the necessary conversions between data and the address of data. To summarize:

&   Returns the address of a variable.
∗   Returns the data pointed to. *by the pointer*

Pointers can be used on both sides of the assignment equation. The statement

```
*ptrx = 10;
```

will set the variable pointed to by **ptrx** to the value 10.

7.2 ARRAYS

Arrays and pointers are closely related in the C language. The compiler converts all array references to pointers internally. The statement

```
int x[10];
```

creates an array of 10 integers named **x**. The elements of this array are **x[0]**, **x[1]**, . . . ,**x[9]**. Note that array indexes start with zero in C. The code

```
for(i=0;i<10;i++)x[i]=10-i;
```

initializes the array **x** to a sequence of numbers from 10 to 1 in descending order. If we now declare an integer pointer

```
int *ptrx;
```

we can use it to address the array. To initialize the pointer, we can use

```
ptrx = &x[4];
```

which sets **ptrx** to the address of the fifth element of the array. The pointer now points to a memory location containing the number 6. If we increment the pointer with the statement

```
ptrx++;
```

it will point to the sixth element of the array, or the number 5. We can use the pointer to access the array by using the indirection operator. The statement

```
y = *ptrx;
```

will set the integer **y** to 5. This has the same effect as

```
y=x[6];
```

In C the name of an array is a pointer constant. As such it can be used as a pointer. The statement

```
ptrx = x;
```

is equivalent to

```
ptrx = &x[0]
```

since the array name is a pointer to the start of the array. This can be somewhat confusing to the uninitiated, since we now have two ways to express the same thing. For example:

```
int point[25];
x = point[6];
```

where we use the array notation, is exactly equal to

```
int point[25];
x = *(point+6);
```

where we are using the pointer notation for the array. In this example, **point** is the address of the start of an array of 25 integers. When we use an expression such as **(point + 6)** we are specifying the address of the seventh integer in the array (**point[0]** is the first element of the array).

When using arrays there is a world of difference between the name of the array and an element in the array. When we declare the character array **name**

```
char name[]="Roberta";
```

the variable **name** is a pointer to a character array, and the variable **name[0]** is a character variable initialized to the letter "R". The variable **name[0]** can also be written *name since the pointer **name** points to the first character of the array. Remember that *name is the variable pointed to by **name**. Carefully note the difference in usage between the name of a string (a pointer) and an element of the string (character). Their usage is completely different, as in

```
printf("%c is the 3rd character of %s.",name[2],name);
```

where we are printing a letter and a string. This can also be expressed as

```
printf("%c is the 3rd character of %s.",name[2],&name[0]);
```

since the address of the first element of an array is the same as the address of the array.

7.3 POINTER AND ARRAY FACTS

The following facts apply to pointers and pointer operations:

1. All pointers are addresses, and they must point to something. Pointers need to be initialized before being used. If a pointer is used before being initialized the results will be indeterminate. This type of mistake can overwrite other data or code.

2. All operations that modify pointers automatically take into consideration the type of variable pointed to. For example, the statement

   ```
   ptr++;
   ```

   will perform a different internal operation depending upon the data type assigned to the variable **ptr**. If **ptr** was declared

   ```
   char *ptr;
   ```

   then the increment will change the address in **ptr** by one byte, the size of a **char** variable. If **ptr** was declared

   ```
   double *ptr;
   ```

   the increment will change the address by eight bytes, the size of a **float**, so that **ptr** points to the next variable of type double.

3. When you are using arrays, you are using pointers. In C, the name of an array is a pointer constant. Array names can be used as pointers, but cannot be modified. The C language supports two sets of terminology for convenience of the programmer, but the results are exactly the same.

4. All strings are arrays of characters. Therefore, all string names are pointers. The declaration

   ```
   char title[25];
   ```

   creates a pointer **title** which points to the beginning of an array of 25 variables of type char. This declaration also reserves space for 25 consecutive variables of type char.

The following statement is a pointer assignment:

```
header = "Total Cost";
```

The pointer **header** is being set to the address of the string constant **Total Cost**. The declaration for the pointer **header** would be

```
char *header;
```

This creates a pointer variable to be used with variables of type char. It does not allocate any storage for characters or initialize the pointer. Storing data with the pointer **header** as the destination before it is initialized could be disastrous.

5. When using arrays be careful not to exceed the bounds of the array. The C run-time system performs no checking on array bounds, so exceeding them can cause a multitude of problems without generating an error message.

7.4 POINTER ARITHMETIC

Pointer variables can be operated on in the same fashion as other variables. The sequence

```
int length;
char name[] = "Donald";
char *nmptr;

nmptr=name+3;
```

is perfectly reasonable. The pointer **nmptr** now points to the fourth element of the array **name**. It is quite common to see pointers used as loop variables as in the code fragment

```
char *name;
char *string;

for(string=name;*string != '\0';string++)
```

where the pointer **string** is being initialized to the pointer **name**, and is then being stepped through the character array until the end of string character ('\0') is encountered. The length of the string can then be calculated by

```
length = string-name;
```

This works because the difference of two pointers is an integer. Note that this can work only when the pointers being used are of the same type.

Some types of pointer arithmetic don't make sense. What is the result of multiplying a pointer? Since pointers are memory addresses, multiplying them makes little sense. The same is true for adding two memory addresses together. The equation

```
nmptr += name;        /* INCORRECT */
```

makes no sense. In general, pointer arithmetic involves setting one pointer equal to another or changing a pointer by an integer amount.

7.5 ARRAY AND POINTER NOTATION

Let's look at an example that uses both array and pointer notation. The program in Figure 7.4 creates an array of 52 "cards," shuffles them, and then prints out the new order.

```
main()
  [
  int cards[52];
  int i;
  int getran();
  int suit,number;
  int ind1,ind2;                      /* indexes into card array for
                                            shuffle sequence */
  int temp;                           /* temp storage for swap */
  char *suitstr[4];
  suitstr[0]="spades";
  suitstr[1]="hearts";
  suitstr[2]="diamonds";
  suitstr[3]="clubs";

  for(i=0;i<52;i++)cards[i]=i;   /* initialize card deck */
  for(i=0;i<500;i++)[                /* shuffle deck by swapping cards
                                        at random */
      temp = cards[ind1=rand()%52];
      cards[ind1]=cards[ind2=rand()%52];
      cards[ind2]=temp;
      }
  for(i=0;i<52;i++){
  suit=cards[i]/13;
  number=cards[i]%13;
  printf("Card %d = %d of %s.\n",i,number,suitstr[suit]);
      }
  }
```

FIGURE 7.4

The first declaration

```
int cards[52];
```

declares the array **cards** and allocates 52 consecutive integer storage locations for it. The statement

```
char *suitstr[4];
```

declares the array **suitstr** and allocates 4 consecutive *pointer* storage locations. By placing the * before **suitstr** we have told the compiler that we are creating an array of pointers. This enables us to proceed with

```
suitstr[0]="spades";
suitstr[1]="hearts";
suitstr[2]="diamonds";
suitstr[3]="clubs";
```

which sets each of the pointers in the array to the address of a string constant. These two operations could be condensed to

```
char *suitstr[4] ={"spades","hearts","diamonds","clubs"};
```

which initializes the pointers at declaration time.

In this example we used the array notation when working with the array cards. The statement

```
cards[ind2]=temp;
```

can also be written as

```
*(cards+ind2)=temp;
```

since **cards** is a pointer. The question quickly arises as to which form is easier to read. The answer to this depends on the application. In the card program, using array notation provides clarity. This is usually true where the operations are being performed directly upon an array declared in the same routine. When functions are working on arrays or strings through passed pointers, the pointer form is often more clear.

The string delete function in the last chapter was written using array notation. We start with the function in Figure 7.5.

```
strngdel(startpos,nchars,string)
int startpos;          /* starting position in string to delete */
int nchars;            /* number of positions to delete */
char string[];         /* string to operate on*/
{
     int length;       /* length of string - calculated */
     int j;
     /* find the length of the string */
     for(length = 0;string[length] != '\0' ; ++length);
     if(startpos > length)
          return(-1); /* starting character beyond end of string */

     for(j = startpos; j < length; j++){
          string[j] = string[j + nchars];
     }
     return(nchars);
}
```

FIGURE 7.5

We then convert it to pointer notation and get the function in Figure 7.6.

```
strngdel(startpos,nchars,string)
int startpos;          /* starting position in string to delete */
int nchars;            /* number of positions to delete */
char *string;          /* string to operate on*/
{
     int length;       /* length of string - calculated */
     /* find the length of the string */
     for(length = 0;*(string+length) != '\0' ; ++length);

     if(startpos > length)
          return(-1); /* starting character beyond end of string */
     for(string = string+startpos ; *string != \0; string++){
          *string = *(string + nchars);
     }
     return(nchars);
}
```

FIGURE 7.6

7.6 MULTIDIMENSIONAL ARRAYS

The C language supports multidimensional arrays with an arbitrary number of dimensions. In practical usage, however, more than three dimensions are rare. The following declaration sets up a status array for disk sectors.

```
#define TRACKS 96
#define SECTORS 16
#define FREE 0
main()
{
int track;
int sector;
int status[TRACKS][SECTORS];
```

The created array has 1536 integer elements (96*16) arranged by rows. To initialize this array

```
for(track=0;track<TRACKS;track++){
   for(sector=0;sector<SECTORS;sector++){
      status[track][sector]=FREE;
      }
}
```

Multidimensional arrays are stored in linear fashion in the computer's memory and it is possible to address them using pointer notation. Elements in multidimensional arrays are grouped from the right-most index inward. This means that if the array is addressed in pointer notation, the right-most index is changing the quickest. In the example above, track 1 sector 1 would be element 17 of the storage array.

7.7 POINTERS TO POINTERS

In the card program, we defined an array of pointers. That array, **suitstr**, consisted of four pointers to strings. Since the name of an array is a pointer constant, **suitstr** is a pointer to pointers. This is a very commonly used data type in C. In C, pointers to pointers can be defined as arrays, as with **suitstr**, or as variables. The declaration

```
char **thissuit;
```

This type of pointer is two levels removed from the actual data (hence the double indirection as part of the declaration). This type of variable must be initialized with the address of a pointer before being used. For example, the sequence of code

```
char *suitstr[4];
char **thissuit;

suitstr[0]="spades";
suitstr[1]="hearts";
suitstr[2]="diamonds";
suitstr[3]="clubs";
    .
    .
    .
thissuit=&suitstr[2];
```

shows **thissuit** ending up pointing to **suitstr[2]** which points to the string **"diamonds"**. To print the string which **thissuit** indirectly points to

```
printf("Current suit = %s\n",*thissuit);
```

This passes **printf** to the pointer pointed to by **thissuit**. In this case the contents of **suitstr[2]** would be passed to **printf** and the string **diamonds** would be printed.

Now that we have constructed a web of variables, let's examine the effects of various operations on the outcomes. The statement

```
thissuit--;
```

will cause **thissuit** to point to the variable **suitstr[1]**. If we then perform the operation

```
suitstr[1]++;
```

we will cause **suitstr[1]** to point to the second character of the string **"hearts"**. If we then perform the operation

```
(*thissuit)++;
```

The variable **suitstr[1]** will be incremented. Look at the program and its output.

```
main()
{
    char *suitstr[4];
    char **thissuit;
    suitstr[0]="spades";
    suitstr[1]="hearts";
    suitstr[2]="diamonds";
    suitstr[3]="clubs";

    thissuit=&suitstr[1];
    printf("Variable thissuit points indirectly to %s.\n"
      ,*thissuit);
    thissuit++;
    printf("After increment it points to %s.\n",*thissuit);
    (*thissuit)++;
    printf("After indirect increment %s.\n",*thissuit);
    (**thissuit)++;
    printf("After double indirect increment %s.",*thissuit);

}
```

FIGURE 7.7

This program prints out as shown below:

```
Variable thissuit points indirectly to hearts.
After increment it points to diamonds.
After indirect increment iamonds.
After double indirect increment jamonds.
```

Follow the sequence of operations in this program which lead to the program printing the word **jamonds**.

The best way to become familiar with pointers is to use them. Try writing test programs such as this one to check out the properties of pointers. It is important when doing this to remember what you are passing to the functions such as **printf**. In this case the **%s** format requires that you pass it a pointer to a string.

Notice that the the indirect increment is performed by (*thissuit)++ rather than *thissuit++. This is because we wish to perform the indirection before the increment, and the two operators have equal precedence. If the other option is used, the pointer **thissuit** will be incremented before the indirection and it will point indirectly to the word **clubs**.

7.8 POINTERS ADDRESSING MEMORY LOCATIONS

When you are writing systems-level programs, it is sometimes necessary to directly access certain memory locations. This is usually caused by the need to directly access hardware locations to determine the state of an interface or to change it. This sort of access is commonly used by operating system programs for input and output functions that must access the keyboard, screen, disk drives, printers, and all of the other peripherals attached to modern computers.

7.9 SUMMARY

The pointer variable allows the C programmer to deal with addresses in a high-level program. The pointers have the advantage of being associated with a specific variable type, so the compiler takes care of the differences in the size of different variables. Lastly, pointers allow C programs to pass data addresses to functions so that the functions can change the data directly. This solves the major problem of call-by-value languages.

Pointers are variables which point to memory locations. Pointers are declared by placing a * before the variable name at declaration. Arrays names are pointer constants. The following facts apply to pointers and arrays:

1. All pointers are addresses, and they must point to something. Pointers need to be initialized before being used.
2. All operations that modify pointers automatically take into consideration the type of variable pointed to.
3. When you are using arrays, you are using pointers. In C, the name of an array is a pointer constant. Array names can be used as pointers, but cannot be modified.
4. All strings are arrays of characters. Therefore, all string names are pointers.
5. When using arrays be careful not to exceed the bounds of the array. The C run-time system performs no checking on array bounds.

REVIEW QUESTIONS

1. What is the relationship between pointers and addresses?
2. What character identifies a pointer declaration?
3. What is the **&** operator used for?
4. Can a pointer be declared without declaring to which data type it points?
5. What is the indirection operator, *, used for?
6. What is the effect of the statement

```
x = *&y;
```

7. How is an array declared?
8. Can doubly subscripted arrays be declared in C?
9. What is the first element of an array in C?
10. Give an example of a pointer constant.
11. What is the difference between a pointer constant and a regular pointer?
12. What is wrong with the following code?

```
int x,*y;
x=3;
y=5;
```

13. What is the relationship between arrays and pointers?
14. What is the effect of adding a constant to a pointer?
15. Can multiplication be performed on pointers?
16. What is wrong with the following code?

```
int x[10];
x[1]=5;
x[10]=10;
```

17. What is the resulting value printed out after this sequence of code?

```
int arr[20];
int i;
int *px,*py;
for(i=0;i<20;i++)arr[i]=i;   initialize 0 to 19
px=&arr[5];
py=&(*px);
printf("Value in py = %d.\n",*py);
```

18. What is the data type of the variable **name** in the following declaration?

```
char *name;
```

19. What is the data type of the variable **name** in the following declaration?

```
char **name;
```

20. Which of the following code segments are legal?
    a. ```
       int *pointer;
       int x;
       pointer = x;
       ```
    b. ```
       int *pointer;
       int x;
       x = pointer;
       ```
    c. ```
       int *pointer;
       int x;
       *pointer = x;
       ```
    d. ```
       int *pointer;
       int x;
       pointer = &x;
       ```
    e. ```
       int *pointer;
       int x;
       x = &pointer;
       ```

21. Which of the following code seqments are legal, but are probably not doing what the programmer intended.
    a. ```
       int *pointer
       int x;
       float y;
       pointer = &x;
       pointer++;
       ```
    b. ```
       int *pointer
       int x[10];
       float y;
       pointer = &x;
       pointer *= 2;
       ```
    c. ```
       int *pointer
       int x[10];
       float y;
       pointer = &x;
       pointer += 5;
       ```
    d. ```
       int *pointer
       int x[10];
       float y;
       pointer = &x;
       pointer += 10;
       ```
       ```

22. In order to read a number from the keyboard with function **scanf** we must pass it a variable name with the address operator. For example:

```
scanf("%d",&number);
```

Why is this neccessary?
23. What is the effect of the double indirection operator (**)?
24. Can pointers be stored in arrays?
25. What is the instruction that will increment the fifth character of the string pointed to by the second element of array **x**?
26. What is the difference in performance between

```
*pointer++;
```

and

```
(*pointer)++;
```

27. Does C monitor the array indices during run time?
28. What is the initial value of the following pointer?

char *pointc;

29. Can pointers be used to address hard-coded memory locations?
30. Why would a program need to address specific memory locations?

PROGRAMMING EXERCISES

1. Modify the card program listed in this chapter so that it prints the correct name of each of the cards. Printed 0 becomes the ace, 12 the king, 11 the queen, and so on.

2. The following function, **chkhnd**, checks the first five cards of the deck for legal poker hands. It currently checks for four of a kind, full house, three of a kind, two pair, and single pair. Add checks for flushes, straights, and straight flushes.

```
chkhnd(deck)
int deck[];
{
    int hand[5];
    int i;
    int j;
    int hits;
    char *hndstr[8]=[
        "no pairs",
        "one pair",
        "two pairs",
        "three of a kind",
        "a full house",
        ".........",
        "four of a kind",
            "........."};

    for(i=0;i<5;i++)hand[i] = deck[i] % 13;
    hits=0;
    for(i=0;i<4;i++){
        for(j=i+1;j<5;j++){
            if(hand[i]==hand[j]hits++;
        }
    }
    printf("Your hand contains %s\n",hndstr[hits]);
    return(hits);
}
```

3. Rewrite the card program to play draw poker. The program should display the user's five-card hand, ask how many the user wishes to replace and which ones to replace, and then replace those cards, and evaluate the hand. You should do a top-down design of the draw-poker program using the techniques demonstrated in the card program.

4. Modify the card program with the hand-checking routine to show the statistical distribution of types of hands over 10,000 hands (do fewer hands if computer time is at a premium). The program should print out a report similar to the report shown on the opposite page.

Type of Hand	Number of Occurrences	%
No pairs	0	0%
One pair	0	0%
Two pairs	0	0%
Three of a kind	0	0%
Straight	0	0%
Flush	0	0%
Full house	0	0%
Four of a kind	0	0%
Straight Flush	0	0%

5. The program below demonstrates a function which copies one string into another. Rewrite the function **strcpy** using pointers. The destination string is initialized in this program to provide verification that the function is properly terminating the destination string.

```
main()
{
      char s1[]="abcdefghijklmn";
      char s2[]="xxxxxxxxxxxxxxx";
      strcpy(s1,s2);
      printf("%s\n",s2);
}
strcpy(src,dst)
char src[];
char dst[];
{
      int i;
      for(i=0;(dst[i]=src[i]) !='\0';i++);
}
```

6. Write a program which will scan a line of text and create an array of words contained in the line. The program should then print out the array.

7. Write a program which will scan an array of integers and summarize the occurrence of each of the ten digits. For example, the following array:

123
900
800
750

would produce the following results:

Digit	Occurrences
0	5
1	1
2	1
3	1
4	0
5	1
6	0
7	1
8	1
9	1

8. Write a function which will scan a block of memory searching for a pattern. The function should accept a pointer to the pattern, which is terminated by a '\0'; a pointer to the block of memory; and an integer specifying the length (in bytes) of the block to search. The function should return a pointer to the beginning of the pattern in the block of memory, or a NUL if no match was found.

9. Write a function which will append one string to another.

10. Write a program which will accept a series of numbers from the user and place them in an ordered array. The function should order the array as they are input, and discard any duplicates.

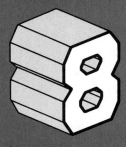

FUNCTIONS
AND PROGRAM
STRUCTURE

LEARNING OBJECTIVES

- Describe the process of defining functions.
- Present the methods of passing arguments to functions.
- Show how functions return values.
- Describe and demonstrate recursion.
- Show how command-line arguments are retrieved.
- Discuss the user interface.

Chapter

FUNCTIONS
AND PROGRAM
STRUCTURE

8.1 FUNCTIONS

The C equivalent of a FORTRAN subroutine or a Pascal procedure is the function. There are three main sources of functions in C programs: user written, system libraries, and custom purchased libraries. No matter the source, the programmer needs to know how to call the function, what types of arguments to pass it, and what type of returns it supplies.

When a C function is defined, the following information is supplied:

1. The data type of the value returned by the function if one is returned.
2. The parameters that are to be passed to the function and the parameter types.
3. The code that makes up the body of the function. This code will be executed when the function is called.
4. The visibility of the function to other code segments in the program.

The format of a function declaration is:

    type function name(parameter list)
    parameter declarations;
    {
         function code
    }

The parameter declarations must match the parameter list in number and type. A simple example is:

```
/* Check to see if the passed character is an alpha
   character.  Return 1 if uppercase, 2 if lowercase
   and -1 if it's a nonalpha character */

int isletter(let2chk)
char let2chk;
{
    if(let2chk >= 'A' && let2chk <= 'Z')return(1);
    if(let2chk >= 'a' && let2chk <= 'z')return(2);
    return(-1);
}
```

FIGURE 8.1

In Figure 8.1, we have declared that the function is type **int**, that its name is **isletter**, and that it accepts one argument, **let2chk**, of type **char**. We have not declared this function as type **static**, so it will be accessible by all other functions linked with it. A function can also be defined so that it is accessible only by functions compiled within the same file by declaring it type **static**.

The type specifier tells the compiler the type of the value returned by the function. The type specifier on a function declaration is optional. If no type is specified when a function is declared, the compiler assigns type **int** to it. If a function does not return a value, it should be declared type **void**.

The function using another function should declare the function type before use. This insures that the variable being assigned the return value from a function is of the correct type. If a function is used without being declared, the compiler assumes that it is of type **int**.

The program in Figure 8.2 tests the **strdel** function. Notice that the main program does not declare the type of function **strdel**. This works fine as long as **strdel** is of type **int**, but when we declare **strdel** as type **void** without reflecting this declaration in the calling function, problems arise.

```
/* Test function strdel.
   **** There is an error in this program.  The function
   strdel is redefined after it is called.  To correct the
   problem add a declaration with type void into main */

main()
{
    char string[26]="ABCDEFGHIJKLMNOP";
    strdel(3,5,string);
    printf("\n%s\n",string);
    }


void strdel(startpos,nchars,string)
int startpos;               /* starting position in string to delete */
int nchars;                 /* number of positions to delete */
char *string;               /* string to operate on*/
{
    int length;             /* length of string - calculated */
    int j;
    /* find the length of the string */
    for(length = 0;*(string+length) != '\0' ; ++length);
    if(startpos < length){
        for(string = string+startpos; *string != '\0'; string++){
            *string = *(string + nchars);
        }
    }

}
```

FIGURE 8.2

When ths program is compiled there will be a type mismatch between the use of **strdel** in **main** and the declaration of **strdel**. This is one of the reasons that many programmers still create most functions as type **int** unless there is a specific requirement to do otherwise.

To correct the problem in the **strdel** test we need to add one line to **main**.

```
main()
{
    char string[26]="ABCDEFGHIJKLMNOP";
    void strdel();

    strdel(3,5,string);
    printf("\n%s\n",string);
}
```

FIGURE 8.3

This declaration notifies the compiler that the function **strdel** is of type **void**. Although many C programmers make every function a type **int**, it is best to declare your functions explicitly. This can save major debugging problems that are caused by not knowing if a function returns a value.

8.2 ARGUMENT PASSING

There are instances where a function can be useful without the calling program providing any arguments, but overall the power of functions lies in performing operations based on one or more passed parameters.

Some examples of useful functions in the system library which do *not* require arguments are **getchar**, **rand**, and **exit**.

In order to make efficient use of C, you must have a clear understanding of the relationships between functions. In programming languages there are two ways of passing arguments to a function or subroutine: call by reference and call by value. Some languages, such as Pascal, allow both of these methods to be used. When an argument is passed by reference, the called routine has direct access to the passed variable and can change it. When arguments are passed by value, a copy of the variable is made for use by the called routine, and the original is kept secure. In C all arguments are passed to functions by value.

With call by value, the variable used as an argument cannot be directly changed by the called function. Instead, the called function is given a copy of the variable, and the copy is discarded when the called function exits. For example, in Figure 8.4 on the opposite page the variable **x** is passed to subroutine **psum** which sums up all of the integers up to and including the passed number.

```
/* Print a running sum of numbers from 1 to 20.
   This is not the most efficient way to do it, but
   it adequately tests function psum.
*/

main()
{
    int x;
    int psum();
    for(x=1;x<=20;x++){
        printf(" %d     %d\n",x,psum(x));
        }
    }

int psum(x)
int x;
{
    int i;
    for(i=x-1;i>0;i--)x +=i;
    return(x);
}
```

FIGURE 8.4

If the value of the original variable **x** was altered by the function, the program would not work. But since **psum** is working only with a copy of **x**, the original is unchanged by the function call.

All arguments are passed to C functions as values, but this fact has different consequences when the argument is a pointer. When a pointer is passed to a function, the original pointer is not changed, but the function is working with a copy of it. This means that the function is still working with a pointer to the real data.

Let's look at a simple sort function. The program in Figure 8.5 sorts an array by checking each element of the array against all following elements and swapping them if the first element is greater than the second. This is not an efficient sorting procedure, but it is one of the easiest to write.

```
/* Test of a quick bubble sort */

main()
{
    int sarray[20];
    int i;
    void bsort();
    for(i=19;i>=0;i--)sarray[i]=i;  /* create test array */
    bsort(sarray,20);
    for(i=0;i<20;i++)printf("%d\n",sarray[i]);
}

/* bsort - perform a quick bubble sort
    enter with    pointer to array of int to sort
                  number of elements to sort
*/
void bsort(array,length)          /* sort in ascending order */
int array[];
int length;
{
    int i,j;
    void swap;

    for(i=0;i<length-1;i++){
        for(j=i+1;j<length;j++){
            if(array[i] > array[j])swap(&array[i],&array[j]);
        }
    }
}

/* swap two integers - enter with two int pointers */
void swap(a,b)
int *a,*b;
{
    int temp;
    temp = *a;
    *a=*b;
    *b=temp;
}
```

FIGURE 8.5

There are two key items to examine in this program. The first is the call to **bsort**. Two values are passed to **bsort**, the pointer constant **sarray** and the integer constant 20. **bsort** is passed a pointer to the beginning of the array. Inside **bsort** this pointer is used to sort the array. Because **bsort** has a pointer to the only copy of the array, using pointers is similar to call by reference (very similar). This technique must be used with extreme care to avoid having functions undermine the data integrity of a program.

The second item to observe is the function **swap**. In order to swap two variables, we must pass addresses of the variables to the function. Passing the values would serve no purpose, since the original variables would remain unchanged.

8.3 RETURNED VALUES

C functions have the option of returning one value. This value can be of any type, as long as the function was properly declared as described above. The value is returned using the **return** statement. The statement form is:

return(expression);

where expression yields the proper type. If no value is to be returned, the function is not required to use a **return** statement. Many functions in C "fall off the end," and this is generally acceptable as long as the function's operation is clearly understandable.

8.4 RECURSION

Recursion in functions is the calling of a function by itself. The function in Figure 8.6 prints a hexadecimal number. If the number received is greater than 15, the function calls itself with the number divided by 16. In this way the highest-order digit is printed first.

```
/* Print a hexadecimal number.  Enter with an integer. */

void hexprnt(num)
int num;
{
    int nxtnum;
    char hexchar[17]={'0123456789ABCDEF'}

    if((nxtnum = num/16) > 0) hexprnt(nextnum);
    printf("%c",hexchar[num%16]);
}
```

FIGURE 8.6

This function will call itself with increasingly smaller numbers until a number less than 16 is found. It will then return back up the line, printing lower-order digits as it goes.

The program in Figure 8.7 tests **hexprint**, and has added print statements to show the program flow.

```
/* test hexprint */
  main()
  {

hexprnt(5000,0);
printf("\n");
  }

  hexprnt(dnum,level)
  int dnum;
  int level;    /* demonstration only -
                  to show depth of recursion */
  {
  int nxtnum;
  char hexchar[17]="0123456789ABCDEF";
        printf ("Entered level %d\n",level);
        if((nxtnum =  dnum/16) > 0) hexprnt(nxtnum,level+1);
        printf("Result at level %d = %c.\n",level,hexchar[dnum%16]);
        printf("Exiting level %d.\n",level);
  }
```

FIGURE 8.7

When the program in Figure 8.7 is run, it will produce the printout in Figure 8.8.

```
Entered level 0.
Entered level 1.
Entered level 2.
Entered level 3.
Result at level 3 = 1.
Exiting level 3.
Result at level 2 = 3.
Exiting level 2.
Result at level 1 = 8.
Exiting level 1.
Result at level 0 = 8.
Exiting level 0.
```

FIGURE 8.8

As you can see, the program descends quickly and then prints the results as it works its way back up the line. Since the digits printed were 1, 3, 8, and 8, the program tells us that 5000 decimal = 1388 hex.

Although recursive routines are often solutions to sloppy problems, they are not without cost. As the level of recursion deepens, the requirements for stack space grow. The large number of function calls also imposes a speed penalty. In conclusion, recursion is an elegant solution, but it is not free from its own problems.

The alternative to this approach is to build an array of characters to print, and then print them in the reverse order of calculation. The **hexprint** function without recursion is shown in Figure 8.9.

```
/* Function hexprint - without using recursion. */

void hexprnt(dnum)
int dnum;
{
    char hexchar[17]="0123456789ABCDEF";
    int i=0;
    char digits[10];
    while(dnum > 0){
        digits[i]=hexchar[dnum%16];
        dnum = dnum/16;
        i++;
    }
    for(dnum=i;dnum>=0;dnum--)printf("%c",digits[dnum]);
}
```

FIGURE 8.9

The resulting function is larger and less elegant, but it uses less stack space and probably runs faster.

8.5 USING RECURSION TO PERFORM A SORT

In the early sixties, C. A. R. Hoare developed the recursive sorting technique known as the **quicksort**. The **quicksort** algorithm works by repetitive partitioning of the list to be sorted into subgroups. The subgroups are segregated into those elements greater than a chosen value and those less than or equal to the chosen value. The partitioning is then applied to the two subgroups. This process continues until all the subgroups are sorted.

A key element of **quicksort** is the choice of the pivot around which the group is divided. The closer to the median value of the array this value is, the more efficient the sort will be.

The **qsort** function is called with a pointer to the data array and the size of the array to sort. The basic structure of **qsort** is:

1. If there is something to sort (size > 1)
   a. Divide the array into two parts (split)
   b. Sort the upper portion with a call to quicksort
   c. Sort the lower portion with a call to quicksort

The real work of sorting is done in Item a, the partitioning of the array. Function **split** is called with a pointer to the beginning of the array to partition, a pointer to the end of the array, and the pivot. The function returns a pointer to the beginning of the upper half of the partition (the calling function already has a pointer to the lower half). The split function can be described this way:

1. While the lower pointer is less than the upper pointer:
   a. Start at the bottom and scan upward until a value is found that is greater than the pivot.
   b. Start at the top and scan until a value is found that is less than or equal to the pivot.
   c. If the lower pointer is less than or equal to the upper pointer, swap the values pointed to.
2. Return the lower pointer

We will perform the swap internal to the split function in order to save the time required for calling the swap function. For simplicity we will choose two values from the array and use the median of those two as the initial pivot point.

The listing of the qsort function with split is shown in Figure 8.10 on the opposite page.

8.6 EXTERNAL VARIABLES

There are times when functions must share a common body of data and the use of pointers for accessing it is too cumbersome, or when a block of data has been defined for access by programs written in different languges. The C language supports the use of **external** data declarations for these needs. However, it is very rare for a new, well-designed program to require the use of externals.

```
/*   qsort - perform quick sort on an integer array
     enter with array and array lenght(int)
*/

qsort(array,length)        /* sort in ascending order */
int *array;
int length;
{
    int *split();
    int *tophalf;
    int pivot;
    if(length>1){
        pivot=((*array+*(array+length-1))/2);
        tophalf=split(array,array+length-1,pivot);
        qsort(array,tophalf-array);
        qsort(tophalf,length-(tophalf-array));
    }
}


/* split - split an array around a given value.
   enter with pointers to the start and end of
   the array and a pivot to split the array
   around (int)
*/


int *split(lowptr,highptr,pivot)
int *lowptr,*highptr;
int pivot;
{
    int temp;
    while(lowptr<=highptr){
        while(*lowptr<pivot)lowptr++;
        while(*highptr>pivot)highptr--;
        if(lowptr<=highptr){
            temp = *lowptr;
            *lowptr=*highptr;
            *highptr=temp;
            lowptr++;
            highptr--;
        }
    }
    return(lowptr);
}
```

FIGURE 8.10

An **external** data area is established by declaring the variables outside of any function to establish storage, and then by declaring them as external inside each function that needs to access them. For example:

```
/* short example of using externals */
int x;
main()
{
external int x;

          .

function2();

          .


}
function2()
{
external int x;

          .
          .
          .

}
```

FIGURE 8.11

It should be noted that using **externals** can be asking for trouble. By allowing any function with an **external** declaration to access the data, you are losing control of the data. Changes made to the data structures at later times can cause unforeseen problems, because there is no easy way of tracing the flow of data from the top down. When pointers are used instead of **externals**, the access to the data can be traced from the highest level to the lowest level relatively easily.

When using **externals** it is wise to place all of the **external** declarations in an **#include** file. This way only one set of changes is required to change all functions accessing the data.

8.7 PUTTING IT TOGETHER AND MOVING CLOSER TO THE REAL WORLD

The C language provides an easy method of getting arguments passed on the command line. When a program is executed, two variables are passed to the main function by the operating system. The first, **argc**, is an integer containing the number of arguments entered on the command line when the command was issued. The second, *argv [], is an array of pointers to the argument strings. The variable *argv[] can also be represented as **argv. The program in Figure 8.12 will copy a text file from the file passed in the first argument to the second.

```
   /* A simple file copy program with a minimum of
error checking.  You should be able to spot at least three
places where this program could be derailed. This version
only works on text files.  You might want to change it to
handle any file.  Check out fread and fwrite functions in
Chapter 10.
*/

/* stdio.h contains all of the i/o equates */
#include <stdio.h>

main(argc,argv)

int argc;
char *argv[];
    {
    FILE *infile;
    FILE *outfile;
    char buffer[80];

    if(argc !=2){  /* In a statement copy a b, the
                   first argument passed the string "a"
                   and the second "b" */

        printf("\nYou must provide two filenames.");
        exit();
        }
    infile=fopen(*argv[0],"r");   /* Open infile in read-only
                                  mode. */
    if(infile == NULL){                /*If we could not open the
                                       file. */
        printf("\nFile %s could not be opened.\n",argv[1]);
        exit();
    }
    outfile=fopen(*argv[1],"w");  /*Open second file in write
                                  mode. */

    while((ch=fgetc(infile)) !=EOF){
        fputc(ch,outfile);
        }
    printf("\nCopy complete\n");
    }
```

FIGURE 8.12

Note that some systems, not UNIX, count the space after a command as the first argument. In that case **argc[1]** and **argc[2]** would contain the file names in the above program.

As a point of interest, take a look at file **stdio.h** on your system. You will find that many of the commonly used system constants are defined, and that special data types, such as **FILE**, are defined using the **typedef** statement. On most systems, the function types of the file-access functions are also declared. This avoids the problem of having the programmer explicitly declare them.

8.8 THE USER INTERFACE

The key element in a program which interacts with a user is the user interface. It is common programming practice to make comments terse within a program and to use jargon within the program. This is fine as long as you do not let it leak out to the user. When dealing with the user of a program follow these rules:

1. Use proper grammar and complete sentences.
2. Give explicit instructions when asking for input. For example, rather than:

    INPUT TEMP

  try:

    Enter the Farenheit temperature and press enter.

  This may seem verbose, but users often find themselves faced with a situation where they simply don't know what to type. If you think this only pertains to novice users, think again. When the experienced user sits down to use a program, he or she probably has to remember four or five common conventions used by commercial programs. This expert user will appreciate the professionalism that never leaves him or her wondering what to type.
3. Try desperately for clean displays. Don't ask for data in the middle of a screen filled with text; don't change the display format from menu to menu; don't fill the screen with extraneous information; don't overload a display.
4. Remain consistent within your program. If you ask for a letter, either require the user to press enter every place in the program where you ask for a letter, or always execute on the keypress.

5. Maintain a consistent escape policy for the user. If pressing the Esc key causes one input routine to return to the previous menu, then all the input routines should follow suit. Advertise the escape policy so the user knows how to get out if he never intended to get there in the first place.

6. Don't do anything irrevocable without double checking. The simple question:

   Do you really want to erase all of your files?

   can save you immense heartache. Also, remember to clear the keyboard buffer before accepting an answer to this type of question.

7. Bury the detail. Structure the user interface so that the top level of menus is a broad overview of capabilities and each submenu delves deeper into the programs specific capabilities. This is sometimes known as "complexity along the Z axis."

8. Write instructions in the user's language. If the program is a financial analysis package, use the terminology of the financial analyst. Don't make the mistake of translating the terminology into your own language and presenting the instructions in your own terms.

8.9 SUMMARY

Functions in C are similar to FORTRAN subroutines or Pascal procedures. When a function is defined, four things are specified:

1. The type and name of the function.
2. The list of arguments passed to the function.
3. The code that makes up the function.
4. The visibility of the function.

C is a call-by-value language, which means that only the values of arguments passed to a function are available to the function. By only passing a value to the function, the variable is safe from modification in the called function. If a variable needs to be changed by a function, there are two options: a pointer to the variable can be passed to the function, or the variable can be declared external. Passing pointers offers far greater control.

Functions can return values to the calling function using the **return** function. The function and the returned value must be of the same type.

C supports recursion, which is a function calling itself. Recursion can provide elegant solutions to some problems, but it imposes a cost in execution speed and stack space.

A good user interface is key to a good program. Some of the rules of a good interface are:

1. Use proper grammar and complete sentences.
2. Give explicit instructions when asking for input.
3. Use clean, uncluttered displays.
4. Remain consistent within your program.
5. Maintain a consistent escape policy for the user.
6. Don't do anything irrevocable without double checking.
7. Bury the detail.
8. Write instructions in the user's language.

If you follow these rules, the program will be easier to use and look more professional.

REVIEW QUESTIONS

1. What is the error in the following code:

```
main()
{
    char *bufptr;

    getline(bufptr);
}

getline(buffer)
char *buffer;
{
    scanf("%s",buffer);
}
```

2. What effect does declaring a function **static** have?
3. What values can be returned by a function of type **void**?
4. What are the three attributes specified when a function is defined?
5. What is the relationship between parameter declarations and the parameter list?
6. Where in the function definition is the parameter list?
7. What separates the parameter declarations and the function code?
8. What is the default function type?

9. What is the relationship between a function's type and the value returned by the function?
10. How does a function return a value?
11. Can a function return without a **return** statement?
12. Name three system library functions that require no parameters.
13. What type of argument is associated with each of the following format specifiers for function **printf**?
    a. %s
    b. %c
    c. %d
    d. %f
14. What are the differences between call by reference and call by value?
15. Is C a call-by-reference or a call-by-value language?
16. What mechanism is used to accomplish the functionality of call by reference?
17. What is the danger of call by reference?
18. How does the function **swap** perform its function if it is called by value?
19. What are the disadvantages of using **externals**?
20. How can the **#include** preprocessor instruction be used to coordinate the use of **externals**?
21. What is recursion?
22. What are the disadvantages of recursion?
23. Are there cases where a function's recursive call to itself is not conditional?
24. Is there a relationship between the call-by-value nature of C and recursion?
25. Where are external variables first declared? Which declaration creates storage for the variable?
26. What is the biggest problem with using external variables?
27. Why is it better to place any external variable definitions in an include file?
28. What are **argv** and **argc** used for?
29. Where are **argv** and **argc** initialized?
30. What data types are **argv** and **argc**?

PROGRAMMING EXERCISES

1. Modify the function **bsort** to accept a parameter which specifies whether the sort is to be in ascending or descending order.
2. Modify the **bsort** function to sort a doubly subscripted array. The function should key on the first column of the array for sorting.
3. Modify function **hexprnt** to accept the base of the number to be printed. The function should accept any base from 1 through 24. You will have to use additional letters for bases greater than 16.
4. Write a recursive function to print a passed string in reverse order. The function will need to pass a modified string pointer to each deeper level. There should be no need to calculate the length of the string to accomplish this. HINT: The function returns if it is passed an empty string.
5. Rewrite the poker program from the last chapter to match the following outline:
   a. Initialize card deck
   b. Game loop – perform forever
      1. Shuffle deck
      2. Display hand
      3. Get discards
      4. Replace discards
      5. Display hand
      6. Check hand and show results

   Implement each item in the outline with a function call whenever possible.
6. Write a recursive function to calculate factorials. The definition of a factorial is:

   n! = n*n-1*n-2...1

   for example:

   4! = 4*3*2*1 = 24 = 4 * 3!   (This is a hint.)

7. Write a nonrecursive function that calculates factorials. Compare the size and speed of the recursive and nonrecursive functions. To test the speed, calculate the same factorial a large number of times and record the CPU time used.

8. Write a program to print the instructions for turning a car around in a driveway. The program must print complete instructions with no conditionals. The program should ask the user all necessary questions including:
   a. Are the keys already in the car?
   b. Is the car an automatic or a standard?
   c. Is the emergency brake set?
   d. Does the car have power steering?
   e. Can the car turn completely without backing?
   When the program has all necessary information it should then print the detailed instructions. Make the user interface clear and explicit!

9. Write a program to accept a number of integer arguments on the command line and print out the max, min, sum, and average of the numbers passed. For example, the command:

   stats 23,45,65,45,45,35,45,45,33,23,12

   will produce:

   minimum   12
   maximum   65
   sum   416
   average   37.82

10. Write a program to accept a decimal argument and print out the ASCII character associated with the value.

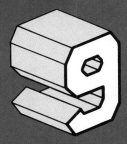

TYPEDEF STATEMENTS AND THE STRUCTURE DATA TYPE

LEARNING OBJECTIVES

- Describe the typedef and structure statements.
- Discuss the use of typedef.
- Cover the definition and use of structures.
- Introduce union data types.
- Introduce the enumeration data type.

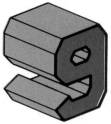

Chapter

TYPEDEF STATEMENTS AND THE STRUCTURE DATA TYPE

9.1 THE TYPEDEF AND STRUCT STATEMENTS

The C language provides methods for creating custom data types. The **typedef** allows the creation of custom type names, and the **struct** allows the creation of data types made up of multiple variables.

9.2 TYPEDEF

The *typedef* statement provides a means of defining new data types. The statement

```
typedef int WHOLE;
```

creates a new data type called **WHOLE** which is equivalent to **int**. After creating this data type, the statement

```
WHOLE numcars;
```

will declare the variable **numcars** to be of type **WHOLE**. If the program requirements change at a later time so that all of the variables of type **WHOLE** were required to handle larger numbers than would fit in an **int**, all that needs to be done is change the **typedef** statement to

```
typedef long WHOLE;
```

which now makes type **WHOLE** equal to type **long**, which will allow larger numbers. The **typedef** does not actually create any new data type, but it can be used to increase the readability of a C program, and it can also make a program easier to maintain or convert to another system.

It is traditional, but not required, to use all capital letters for data types created with the **typedef** statement. This stops custom types from becoming confused with standard types.

9.3 STRUCTURES

NOTE: The level of support for structures varies from compiler to compiler. The simplest form of support does not allow the assignment of structures, passing of structures to functions, or returning of structures by functions. Most modern compilers have lifted these restrictions, and complete support for structures will be standard in the future. Check your compiler manual for the level of support it offers. This chapter will cover some areas not supported by all compilers. If you are writing programs which will need to converted to other compilers and other machines, it is best to avoid using these features.

Structures in C are similar to records in Pascal. Structures are a way of creating a variable which contains multiple pieces of information, usually of multiple data types.

The code in Figure 9.1 is a common sequence often seen in programs. The code creates a set of parallel arrays to store the test data for a class.

```
main()
{
char names[20][12];    /* 20 names - 12 characters each */
int scores[20][4];     /* 20 students - 4 tests each */
int average[20];       /* 20 students - average for each */
```

FIGURE 9.1

This sequence creates a set of records for the class. The code in Figure 9.2 prints the data for student six.

```
printf("Name - %s\n",name[6]);
prints("Scores - %d   %d   %d   %d \n",
    scores[6][0],scores[6][1],scores[6][2],scores[6][3]);
printf("Average - %d\n",average[6];
```

FIGURE 9.2

The structure data type offers an alternative to parallel arrays. With structures, a new data type can be created which contains all pertinent data for the student. In C the structure for the student data would be defined

```
struct student{
    char name[20];
    int scores[4];
    int average;
    };
```

FIGURE 9.3

We can then define an array of 20 students by

```
struct student class[20];
```

which creates an array named **class** which has 20 elements of type **struct student**. The code to print array element six is shown in Figure 9.4.

```
printf("Name - %s\n",class[6].name);
prints("Scores - %d   %d   %d   %d \n",
    class[6].scores[0],class[6].scores[1],
    class[6].scores[2],class[6].scores[3]);
printf("Average - %d\n",class[6].average;
```

FIGURE 9.4

This is more wordy, but it is clear what the program is doing.

9.4 DEFINING STRUCTURES

Let's look at one example of a structure. The structure in Figure 9.5 is for inspection of parts in a manufacturing operation. In order to inspect a part, the operator needs to know the part number, the revision letter, the feature to inspect, the expected value, the minimum acceptable value, and the maximum acceptable value.

```
struct inspect{
    char partnum[10];
    char revlet;
    char feature[22];
    int expected;
    int min;
    int max;
    };
```

FIGURE 9.5

We have now created a structure type named **inspect** that contains six elements. We have not yet declared any variables to be used with this structure. The structure **inspect** is just a description, or template of the structure. To use this structure we will declare variables for two of the inspection stations. We declare these variables by

struct inspect cordax1,cordax2;

which declares variables **cordax1** and **cordax2** to be structures of type **inspect**. Variables can also be defined at the time of structure creation as in Figure 9.6.

```
struct inspect{
    char partnum[10];
    char revlet;
    char feature[22];
    int expected;
    int min;
    int max;
    }cordax1,cordax2;
```

FIGURE 9.6

This creates two variables, **cordax1** and **cordax2**. The structure name, **inspect**, is optional. If the only variables that are being declared are listed after the structure definition, there is no need for the structure name. This allows the third option, as shown in Figure 9.7.

```
struct {
     char partnum[10];
     char revlet;
     char feature[22];
     int expected;
     int min;
     int max;
     }cordax1,cordax2;
```

FIGURE 9.7

This declares **cordax1** and **cordax2**, but does not create a new type to be used in later declarations.

These three ways of declaring structures all have the same end effect of creating the two variables **cordax1** and **cordax2**. The type of structure declaration is largely a matter of taste, and a question of how many variables are being defined of that structure type.

The names used as members of a structure can be used to declare other variables outside the structure without causing an error. For example:

```
struct inspect{
     char partnum[10];
     char revlet;
     char feature[22];
     int expected;
     int min;
     int max;
     }cordax1,cordax2;

int min,max;
```

FIGURE 9.8

The code in Figure 9.8 declares two integer variables **min** and **max** which have nothing to do with the variables **cordax1.min**, **cordax2.min**, **cordax1.max**, and **cordax2.max**. This "feature" of C should be used with extreme caution since it can easily prove confusing. When at all possible a clear distinction should be made between members of a structure and other variables in the program.

9.5 ADDRESSING STRUCTURES

Now that we have declared these variables, we need to be able to address the structure members. A member of a structure is referenced by its structure name and its member name with a period separating them. The statement

```
cordax1.min = 4;
```

sets the member **min** of structure **cordax1** to the value 4. The statement

```
if(cordax2.partnum[6] = 'F')  . . . . .
```

checks the seventh character of the **partnum** variable of **cordax2**.

9.6 INITIALIZING STRUCTURES

A structure of type **external** or **static** can be initialized at declaration. For example:

```
struct error {
    char *descrip;
    char *chapter;
};

static struct error probtab [7] = {
    "no error","xxx",
    "double negative","glossary",
    "spelling (there/their)","glossary",
    "usage (a lot/alot)","glossary",
    "usage (accept/except)","glossary",
    "noun as adjective","5b",
    "correlative conjunction","5d",
    }
```

FIGURE 9.9

The code sequence in Figure 9.9 creates a structure type **error** and then initializes the array of structures, **probtab**. This is equivalent to the sequence in Figure 9.10 on the opposite page.

```
struct error {
    char *descrip;
    char *chapter;
};
    struct error probtab [7];

probtab[0].descrip = "no error";
probtab[0].chapter = "xxx";
probtab[1].descrip = "double negative";
probtab[1].chapter = "glossary";
probtab[2].descrip = "spelling (there/their)";
probtab[2].chapter = "glossary";
probtab[3].descrip = "usage (a lot/alot)";
probtab[3].chapter = "glossary";
probtab[4].descrip = "usage (accept/except)";
probtab[4].chapter = "glossary";
probtab[5].descrip = "noun as adjective";
probtab[5].chapter = "5b";
probtab[6].descrip = "correlative conjunction";
probtab[6].chapter = "5d";
```

FIGURE 9.10

Either sequence leaves the program with an array of structures initialized to a set of error messages and chapter numbers. The function can now use a single index to access the error message and corresponding chapter.

9.7 ARRAYS OF STRUCTURES

Structures can be treated like most other data types. The sequence in Figure 9.11 creates two arrays of structures, **plot1** and **plot2**.

```
struct complex {
    double real;
    float imag;
    }
struct complex plot1[100],plot2[100];
```

FIGURE 9.11

Both of these arrays contain 100 structures. To address the **real** portion of the fourth structure of array **plot1**, use the statement

```
x = plot1[3].real;
```

Arrays of structures are often used in more complex data structures such as linked lists. We will cover these in detail in the next chapter.

9.8   STRUCTURE ASSIGNMENT

Most modern C compilers allow the assignment of structures. For example:

```
struct inspect{
    char partnum[10];
    char revlet;
    char feature[22];
    int expected;
    int min;
    int max;
    };

struct inspect cordax1,cordax2;
    .
    .
    .
cordax2 = codax1;
```

FIGURE 9.12

In this sequence we have "copied" structure **cordax1** into **cordax2**. This is equivalent to the sequence in Figure 9.13.

```
struct inspect{
    char partnum[10];
    char revlet;
    char feature[22];
    int expected;
    int min;
    int max;
    };
```

FIGURE 9.13   *(Part 1 of 2)*

```
struct inspect cordax1,cordax2;
        .
        .
        .
strcpy(cordax2.partnum,cordax1.partnum);
cordax2.revlet = cordax1.revlet;
strcpy(cordax2.feature,cordax1.feature);
cordax2.expected = cordax1.expected;
cordax2.min = cordax1.min;
cordax2.max = cordax1.max;
```

FIGURE 9.13   *(Part 2 of 2)*

Obviously the simpler form is preferable.

9.9 NESTED STRUCTURES

The C language supports the nesting of structures and the recursive use of structures. Suppose we wish to create a database that describes a company's structure. The smallest unit would be a person. The structure declaration for a person is shown in Figure 9.14.

```
struct person{
    char lastname[20];
    char firstname[11];
    char midinit;
    char badge[12];
    int rank;
    int location;
    }
```

FIGURE 9.14

This structure contains all of the pertinent information for the company structure. The next higher level of company structure, the group, is declared in Figure 9.15 on the following page. There can be no more than six employees in a group.

```
struct group{
     char groupname[20];
     struct person gleader;
     struct person gmember[6];
     }
```

FIGURE 9.15

The next level of company structure, the department, is declared in Figure 9.16.

```
struct department{
     char depname[20];
     struct person manager;
     struct group depgroup[12];
     }
```

FIGURE 9.16

As you can see, we quickly build an inverted tree with the top-most structure type being the company and the lowest being the person. To address a person's last name from the group level, we need to chain down the tree. To get to group member 3 of group 5 the statement

```
depgroup[5].gmember[3].lastname
```

uniquely specifies the last name of the person in question.

Pointers in C work on structures in the same way as with other variable types. All operations on pointers to structures allow for the size of the structure. The address of a structure can be obtained using the address operator, **&**. The code segment in Figure 9.17 creates structure type **person**, declares an array of five **person**s named **employee**, and assigns the address of the third **employee** to the pointer **pstruct**.

Once **pstruct** is declared, the statement

```
pstruct++;
```

will set **pstruct** to the address of the fourth **employee**. To access the member **rank** of this structure, we must use the structure pointer operator, **->**.

```
currentrank = pstruct->rank;
```

```
struct person{
     char lastname[20];
     char firstname[11];
     char midinit;
     char badge[12];
     int rank;
     int location;
     }employee[5];
struct person *pstruct;
     .
     .
     .
pstruct = &employee[2];
```

FIGURE 9.17

This is equivalent to

```
currentrank = (*pstruct).rank;
```

which uses the indirection operator to get the value pointed to by **pstruct** and then combine it with **rank**.

Pointers can also point to individual members of a structure. For example:

```
*prank = &employee[2].rank;
```

sets the pointer **prank** to the address of the member **rank** of the third structure in the array **employee**. In this case, the pointer must be of the same type as the member to which it points. This type of pointer is not a structure pointer; it is of the more mundane **int** variety.

9.10 UNIONS

The **union** data type is designed to avoid a common problem in computer programming, namely that you can't always be sure that a constant data type will be used to specify a value. The **union** is really a special type of structure in which each element occupies the same space, and space is allocated for the largest member. For example, the sequence in Figure 9.18 on the following page defines a variable, mycolor, that can be used to store either an integer or a character pointer.

```
union color{
    int colval;
    char *coltxt;
    }mycolor;
```

FIGURE 9.18

The variable will be large enough to hold the largest specified type. The variables are addressed exactly as in structures.

```
mycolor.colval = 23;
```

It is the responsibility of the programmer to keep track of which data type is currently stored in a union.

When you are using unions, certain problems will arise when the variable is passed to other functions. In these cases you will need to translate the data explicitly into the data type expected by the function. If, with the union above, you have associated a variable, **mycoltype**, which you have carefully set to values of **INT** or **STRING** whenever data is stored in **mycolor**, then to print **mycolor** we would use the sequence in Figure 9.19.

```
    mycolor.colval = 23;
    mycoltype = INT;              /* INT is #defined */
        .
        .
    if(mycoltype == STRING){
        printf("The color is %s",mycolor.coltxt);
        }
    if(mycoltype == INT){
        printf("The color is %d",mycolor.colval);
        }
```

FIGURE 9.19

As you will undoubtedly note, there are other ways of solving the problems for which unions are used. In this case, we could have designed the program so that it always worked with character pointers and always printed strings. This requires some work when the data is input, but usually simplifies things in the long run.

9.11 ENUMERATION TYPES

The enumeration data type creates a set of values and associates names with them. These names, or enumeration constants, then can be used with all variables defined as that enumeration type. For example, the statement

```
enum size{xsmall=34,small=36,medium=38,large=40,xlarge=44};
```

creates an enumeration type named **size** and a set of enumeration constants, xsmall, small, and so on. We can declare variables of this type

```
enum size purchased, returned, newsize;
```

We can also assign values to these variables using the enumeration constants

```
purchased = medium;
returned = large;
```

and we can use the enumeration constants in **if** statements, such as

```
if(returned == xlarge)
```

If the specific values of the enumeration constants are not important, we can allow the system to assign them

```
enum colors{red, orange, yellow, green, blue, indigo,
      violet};
```

and variables can be declared in combination with declaring the enumeration type

```
enum colors{red, orange, yellow, green, blue, indigo,
      violet}firstcol, secondcol, finalcol;
```

In most compilers, enumeration types are implemented as integers, and programmers occasionally treat them as such. Most compilers will issue warning messages in these cases, but will allow the code to run. When using enumeration types, try to keep the code pure.

Once you have defined the enumeration types, program maintenance becomes much easier. For instance, in the first example all that is necessary to change a size is to change the value in the enumeration list.

9.12 SUMMARY

The C language provides four means of creating special data types. They are:

1. The **typedef** statement.
2. The structure construct.
3. The **union** statement.
4. The **enum** statement.

The **typedef** statement allows the programmer to define new types in terms of existing C types. This is very useful when groups of variables need to be changed at some later point. The statement

```
typedef int WHOLE;
```

creates a new data type called **WHOLE** which is equivalent to **int**.

C permits the programmer to group related variables of different types into one variable, a structure. Once a structure type is defined, it can be used much the same as any other type of variable. The sequence

```
struct car{
     int year;
     char name[20];
     }
```

creates type **car**, which is a structure with members **year** and **name**. If variable **mycar** is of type **car**, we can address the member **year** with the variable name **mycar.year**. With a pointer, **yourcar**, to structure of type **car**, the year is addressed with the variable name **yourcar->year**. C supports arrays of structures and nested structures.

The **union** is used in cases where the type of the data to be stored in a variable is not known. Space is reserved for the longest possible variable type. It is the responsibility of the programmer to keep track of what variable type is stored in the **union** and to make any necessary conversions when passing the variable to functions. For example:

```
union color{
     int colval;
     char *coltxt;
     };
```

creates type **color**, which can store either an integer or a character pointer.

The enumeration data type creates a set of values, and associates names with them. These names, or enumeration constants, can then be used with all variables defined as that enumeration type. Values can be assigned to the enumeration values, or you can allow the compiler to automatically assign values. For example:

```
enum size
    {xsmall=34,small=36,medium=38};
```

creates a type, **size**, which can have the values **xsmall**, **small**, or **medium**.

These added data types create the needed flexibility for structured and modular programming in C.

REVIEW QUESTIONS

1. What are the advantages of using **typedef** statements?
2. Why are capital letters used for types created with the **typedef**?
3. The **FILE** type is created by a **typedef** in **stdio.h**. What is the definition of a **FILE** type?
4. Can **typedef** be used to create a type which is a pointer to a structure?
5. Is the folowing statement legal?

   typedef char;

6. What is wrong with the following sequence?

   #define strsiz
   typedef char* string

7. What is the type of **house.color** in the following example?

```
struct{
    char *type;
    char *location;
    int size;
    int color;
    }house;
```

8. What is wrong with the following sequence?

```
struct{
    char *location;
    int size;
    };
```

9. What data type is **ourcar** in the following sequence?

```
struct car{
    char *model;
    int year;
    char *color;
    };
struct car *ourcar;
```

10. What will be printed in the following sequence?

```
struct car{
    char *model;
    int year;
    char *color;
    };
struct car *ourcar;

struct car{
    char *model;
    int year;
    char *color;
    }lotcars[20];
struct car *ourcar;

for(i=1;i<20;i++){
    lotcars[i].year=88;
    }
ourcar=&lotcars[2];
printf("The answer is %d.",ourcar.year);
```

11. What will be printed in the following sequence?

```
struct car{
    char *model;
    int year;
    char *color;
    };
struct car *ourcar;
```

continued

```
struct car{
    char *model;
    int year;
    char *color;
    }lotcars[20];
struct car *ourcar;

for(i=1;i<20;i++){
    lotcars[i].year=65+i;
    }
ourcar=&lotcars[0];
printf("The answer is %d.",ourcar->year);
```

12. Once again, what will be printed at the end of the sequence?

```
struct car{
    char *model;
    int year;
    char *color;
    };
struct car *ourcar;

struct car{
    char *model;
    int year;
    char *color;
    }lotcars[20];
struct car *ourcar;

for(i=1;i<20;i++){
    lotcars[i].year=88;
    }
ourcar=&lotcars[2];
ourcar +=2;
printf("The answer is %d.",ourcar.year);
```

13. Is the following sequence correct?

```
typedef struct{
    char *model;
    int year;
    char *color;
    }CAR;
CAR lotcars[20];
```

14. What is wrong in the following sequence?

```
typedef struct{
     char *model;
     int year;
     char *color;
     }CAR;
CAR lotcars[20];
CAR[19].year=87;
```

15. What is wrong with the following sequence?

```
struct car{
     char *model;
     int year;
     char *color;
     struct car lotcars[10];
     };
```

16. What is wrong with the following sequence?

```
struct car{
     char *model;
     int year;
     char *color;
     struct car *oldcar;
     }ourcar;
struct lotcars[20];

ourcar = lotcar[10];
ourcar.oldcar=oldcar[5];
```

17. Comment on the legality of the following sequence:

```
struct car{
     char *model;
     int year;
     char *color;
     struct car *oldcar;
     }ourcar;
struct lotcars[20];

ourcar = lotcar[10];
ourcar.oldcar=&ourcar;
```

18. What is the operator –> used for?
19. What is the alternative to using the –> operator?

20. What is wrong with the following sequence?

```
char test(data)
struct{
      int test1;
      int test2;
      }data;
{
      data->test1 = 123;
}
```

21. What is a union?
22. What is the size of a union variable?
23. How do you know what data type is stored in a union variable?
24. Why doesn't the following make sense?

```
union mix{
      int mix1;
      int mix2;
      int mix3;
      };
```

25. What is the **enum** declaration used for?
26. How are values assigned to enumeration constants?
27. What is wrong with the following sequence?

```
enum color{red = 1, orange = 3, yellow = 2, green = 1,
      blue = 2, indigo = 5, violet = 6};
```

28. Is the following code legal?

```
enum fish{cod,bluefish,bass}activefish;
activefish=2;
```

29. What is the advantage of using enumeration types?
30. What is the data type of enumeration constants on most systems?

PROGRAMMING EXERCISES

1. Write a function to print error codes for an on-line programming test. Each error has an error description associated with it, a lesson number, and type code. The list at the top of the next page shows error codes.

Error Code	Description	Lesson	Type
1	Assignment Syntax error	2	A
2	Declaration Syntax error	2	A
3	Type mismatch	3	B
4	Mismatched quotes	4	C
5	No statement terminator	5	C
6	Undefined variable reference	6	C
7	Illegal function call	7	D
8	Argument mismatch	8	E

2. Write a function similar to **bsort** from the previous chapter which sorts an array of structures based on a key field. The structure definition is

```
struct sortrec{
    int keyfield;
    char name[20];
    char address[60];
    int age;
    }
```

3. Write a set of functions which operate on complex numbers. The complex number should be passed to the function as a structure, and each function should return a complex value.

4. Write a program to maintain a phone list. The list should be stored in an internal array of structures. Each structure should contain a first name, last name, area code, and phone number. There should be functions for adding, deleting, and printing phone numbers.

5. If your system supports color displays, write a set of functions for printing characters in color. Use the **typedef** statement to define all of the constants required for the program.

6. Enter and execute the program at the top of the next page onto your system. What does the result tell you about your compiler's handling of enumeration types?

```
main()
{
enum test{val1 = 1, val2 = 2, val3 = 4, val4 = 6,
     val5 = 100}testvar1;

testvar1 = val1;
printf("\ntestvar1 = %d   - should be 1.\n",testvar1);
testvar1++;
printf("\ntestvar1 = %d after ++, should be 2",testvar1);
testvar1++;
printf("\ntestvar1 = %d after second ++, should be 4",testvar1);
testvar1 += 2;
printf("\ntestvar1 = %d after += 2, should be 100",testvar1);
}
```

If this program comes up with values of 1, 2, 3 and 5, you know that your compiler does not really support enumeration types, since the values do not match the enumeration list. If the program comes up with 1, 2, 4 and 100, you know that enumeration types are completely supported.

PROGRAMMING PROJECT – C PROGRAM RETAB

A common problem encountered when developing programs in C happens when a major change is made to the program. At that point it is very difficult to match the programs indenting with the the program structure. We need a program to process source files and fix the indentation. For example, let us start with the following program:

```
char menu()
{
     char choice = 0;
     clrscrn();              /* compiler dependant function
                               to clear the screen */
     printf("\n\n Select from the following options.");
     printf("\n\n     A. Setup the program.");
     printf("\n\n     B. Acquire and screen data.");
     printf("\n\n     C. Print the run report.");
     printf("\n\n     X. Exit the program.");
     printf("\n\n Enter your choice (A,B,C or X).   ");
```

continued

```
    choice = getchar();
    choice = choice & 0xdf;
    if(choice <'A' || (choice > 'C' && choice != 'X')){
        beep();
        printf("\n\n You must select A, B, C or X");
        choice = getchar();
        choice=0;
    }
    return(choice);
}
```

Now we add an outer loop that requires that the choice be legal before this routine will exit.

```
char menu()
{
    char choice = 0;
    while(choice == 0){
    clrscrn();              /* compiler dependant function
                                to clear the screen */
    printf("\n\n Select from the following options.");
    printf("\n\n    A. Setup the program.");
    printf("\n\n    B. Acquire and screen data.");
    printf("\n\n    C. Print the run report.");
    printf("\n\n    X. Exit the program.");
    printf("\n\n Enter your choice (A,B,C or X).   ");
    choice = getchar();
    choice = choice & 0xdf;
    if(choice <'A' || (choice > 'C' && choice != 'X')){
        beep();
        printf("\n\n You must select A, B, C or X");
        choice=0;
    }
    }
    return(choice);
}
```

Now the indentation does not match the program's structure. We need a program that takes the above program and produces a file with the indentation corrected, such as

```
char menu()
{
    char choice = 0;
    clrscrn();              /* compiler dependant function to
                                clear the screen */
```

continued

```
while(choice == 0){
    printf("\n\n Select from the following options.");
    printf("\n\n     A. Setup the program.");
    printf("\n\n     B. Acquire and screen data.");
    printf("\n\n     C. Print the run report.");
    printf("\n\n     X. Exit the program.");
    printf("\n\n Enter your choice (A,B,C or X).   ");
    choice = getchar();
    choice = choice & 0xdf;
    if(choice <'A' || (choice > 'C' && choice != 'X')){
        beep();
        printf("\n\n You must select A, B, C or X");
        choice=0;
        }
    }
return(choice);
}
```

The retab program will follow a simple algorithm:

1. If the line ends with a semicolon, the tabbing level remains the same; if it ends with anything else, the tab level increases.
2. If a line ends with a right bracket (}) the tabbing level decreases.
3. If the previous line ended without either a semicolon or a left bracket ({), and the current line ends with a semicolon, the tabbing level decreases. This handles the line

```
printf("This is a test line with 4 arguments %d %d %d %d."
    arg1,arg2,arg3,arg4);
```

A problem arises with some statement types, such as:

```
mainmenu();
clearkbd();
x=getkey(&choice);
switch(choice){
    case 'A':
        if((x=designtst()) != -1)test();
        endflg=0;
        break;
    case 'B':
        if(loadtst() != -1)test();
        endflg=0;
        break;
```

continued

```
case 'C':
     x=reviewchp();
     break;
case 'D':
     x=editchp();
     break;
case 'E':
     edithdr(1);
     break;
case hlpkey:
     help1();
     break;

case ESC:
     endflg=1;
     break;
default:
     beep();
     break;
}       /* end of main loop switch */
```

The **case** statement, and the labels for **goto** statements, will have to be handled as a special case.

Additional features of the program should include error checking for mismatched parentheses and brackets ({ }).

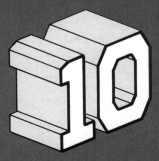

DATA STRUCTURES IN C

LEARNING OBJECTIVES

- Introduce dynamic memory allocation.
- Describe and demonstrate the use of stacks in C.
- Describe and demonstrate the use of buffers in C.
- Describe and demonstrate the use of linked lists in C.
- Describe and demonstrate the use of trees in C.

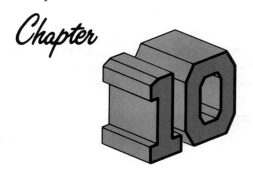

Chapter 10

DATA STRUCTURES IN C

10.1 DATA STRUCTURES IN C

The handling of information is key to computer programs of any language. The increasing capability of computers has made it possible to process and store more information than ever before. As the amount of information and the complexity of interrelationships among data grows, the task of handling and storing the data becomes more complex.

To aid the programmer, there are some common techniques for handling data which make this task more manageable and make the program's data management more efficient. Both the application and the structure of the data will determine the best method of representing the data within your program. We will examine some of these techniques as they relate to the more common data structures.

10.2 DYNAMIC MEMORY ALLOCATION

All data structures have one thing in common: They occupy space. Before creating these data structures and filling them with data, you must allocate space for them in the program. The easiest way to accomplish this is to define an array of the proper data types.

If the data is a list of 1000 integers, the statement

```
int list[1000];
```

will allocate the necessary space. This works well when the size of the data is known, or it is not too large. When the amount of data grows too large to be conveniently built into the code, or the amount of space required is not a constant, the program must obtain the space from the operating system during execution. This is called dynamic memory allocation. There are three functions required to allocate memory dynamically: **sizeof** returns the memory size of a variable; **malloc** allocates memory; and **free** releases memory back to the system.

The **sizeof** function returns the size of the argument. The code

```
struct client{
     char name[20];
     char address[60];
     char zipcode[10];
     int age;
     };
int structsz
     .
     .
     .

structsz = sizeof(struct client);
```

sets the variable **structsz** to number of bytes occupied by a structure of type **client**.

The function **malloc** is called to allocate a sequential block of memory to a program. The amount of memory required is passed to **malloc** and a pointer to the memory block is returned. The code

```
struct client{
     char name[20];
     char address[60];
     char zipcode[10];
     int age;
     };
```

continued

```
int structsz
char *malloc();
struct client *user;        /* pointer to user */
  .
  .
  .

structsz = sizeof(struct client);
user = malloc(sizeof*20) /* get memory for 20 user records */
```

creates the structure type, **client**, and then allocates memory for 20 records of that type. The variable **user** points to the beginning of this space. The space can later be released by the statement

```
free(user);
```

It is good programming practice to check the value returned by **malloc**. If **malloc** is unable to allocate the requested memory, the value **NULL** will be returned. Knowing that there is a problem allows you to arrange an orderly exit with the minimum loss of data.

10.3 STACKS

Stacks are among the most common data structures encountered in computer programming. Data stacks are analogous to physical stacks of objects. Data stacks follow the same basic rules as physical stacks, such as a stack of books. Objects are always added at the top of the stack and removed from the top of the stack, making stacks a last-in-first-out, or LIFO, data structure. The least accessible object is at the bottom of the stack. Once the bottom object is removed, the stack is empty.

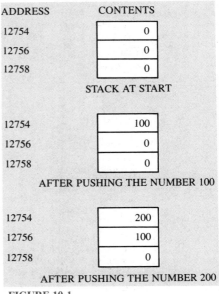

FIGURE 10.1

Stacks can be used with either dynamic or static memory systems, but stacks must reside in a contigous segment of memory. When dealing with stacks, it is customary to use the term **push** to denote placing data onto the stack and **pop** to denote removing data from the stack.

Stacks are among the most common of data structures. Most microprocessors have stack manipulation instructions built into the hardware, and most computer languages use stacks for passing arguments to functions and for preserving registers during function execution.

Stacks are ideally suited for program control-type functions because they address the basic need of programs which have multiple levels of functions. Before control is passed to a lower level, the volatile data (usually registers) is saved on the stack and the arguments are placed on the stack. The called function then removes the arguments from the stack and executes. As control is passed back up levels, each level finds its volatile data on the top of the stack.

The major requirement in using stacks is discipline. Each function using the stack must leave the stack in the proper condition. All passed arguments must be removed, and no extraneous garbage can be left on the stack. Once a stack is corrupted, program control degrades quickly.

The structure in Figure 10.2 defines a stack. All data "pushed" onto, or "popped" off of the stack is handled a character (byte) at a time.

```
struct stack{
    char *bottom;
    char *top;
    int maxsize;            /* (top - bottom) must be <= maxsize */
    };
```

FIGURE 10.2

The stack type structure requires that space be allocated for it. To set up a stack that can hold the equivalent of 200 integers, use the code in Figure 10.3.

```
struct stack{
    char *bottom;
    char *top;
    int maxsize;            /* (top - bottom) must be <= maxsize */
    }userstack;
    userstack.top = userstack.bottom = malloc(sizeof(int)*200);
    userstack.maxsize = 200;
```

FIGURE 10.3

Once executed, this program will have created an empty stack with room for 200 integer variables. The variable **userstack.top** will always point to the next open space. When **userstack.top** is equal to **userstack.bottom** the stack is empty. When **userstack.top** minus **userstack.bottom** equals **maxsize** the stack is full. If this were a real program, we would have defined the stack size rather than hard-coding it.

In order to use the stack we need a mechanism for placing data on it and removing data from it. We will write two routines, **push** and **pop** to accomplish these tasks. In order to operate the routines, we need the stack structure (or a pointer to it), a pointer to the variable, and the size of the variable.

```
typedef struct stack{
     char *bottom;
     char *top;
     int maxsize;            /* (top - bottom) must be <= maxsize */
     };
#define STACKSIZE 200;
main()
{
struct stack userstack;
char *malloc();
userstack.top = userstack.bottom = malloc(sizeof(int)*STACKSIZE);
userstack.maxsize = STACKSIZE;
push(&userstack,test,sizeof(test));
pop(&userstack,test2,sizeof(test2));

}
/*  Push - push data onto the stack
    enter with pointer to stack, pointer to data, and
    integer specifying number of bytes to push
*/

push(wrkstack,data,datasize)
struct stack *wrkstack;
char *data;
int datasize;
{
int i;
for(i=0;i<datasize;i++){
    *wrkstack->top++ = *data++;
    }
}
/*  Pop - pull data off the stack
    enter with pointer to stack, pointer to data, and
    integer specifying number of bytes to pull
*/
```

FIGURE 10.4 *(Part 1 of 2)*

```
pop(wrkstack,data,datasize)
struct stack *wrkstack;
char *data;
int datasize;
{
int i;
for(i=datasize-1;i>=0;i--){
     *(data+i) = *--wrkstack->top;
     }
}
```

FIGURE 10.4   *(Part 2 of 2)*

Notice that the stack structure type in Figure 10.4 is a **typedef**. This allows all of the routines compiled together to use the **stack** data type.

10.4 BUFFERS AND QUEUES

Buffers and queues are data structures where data is removed in the same order as it is added to the structure. This is known as a FIFO, or first-in-first-out, list. A real-life analogy to a queue is the cafeteria line. Data is always added to the queue at the top and removed from the bottom.

Let's examine some situations where buffers and queues are required.

a. A program which accepts input from the keyboard and updates a display, such as a word processing program, has an average processing rate far beyond the rate at which a user can enter data. The problem arises in special cases where the program consumes a relatively large amount of processing time after an input. Since the program does not wish to lose user input, the keyboard must be buffered. The size of the buffer can be small, but without it the program would occasionally miss a character.

b. A user program generally reads data from a disk in units sized by the data type, but the system must read the data based on the physical constraints of the hardware. To solve this problem, operating systems use circular buffers to insulate the user program from the physical constraints imposed by the hardware. The user can then read a character at a time and the system will deliver a character from the buffer. When the buffer is empty, the system will read in another block of data from the disk.

c. It is necessary for some programs to work with real-world situations where real-world buffers and queues are present. These programs could be dealing with anything from airline scheduling to print buffering. These programs use buffers to replicate the real-world situation.

There are two ways of managing FIFO data storage. The least efficient is to place data at the top and to move the stack down when data is removed from the bottom. An alternative is to form a circular buffer with floating pointers for data in and data out. We will examine the circular buffer.

The circular buffer requires four pointers for its maintenance: top, which delimits the top of the buffer; bottom, which delimits the bottom; in, which marks where the next data is to be stored; and out, which points to the next available data.

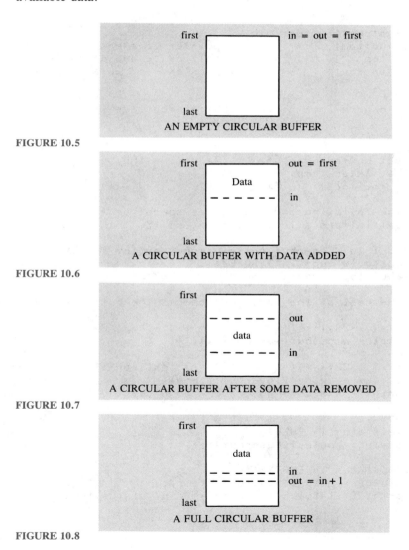

FIGURE 10.5

AN EMPTY CIRCULAR BUFFER

FIGURE 10.6

A CIRCULAR BUFFER WITH DATA ADDED

FIGURE 10.7

A CIRCULAR BUFFER AFTER SOME DATA REMOVED

FIGURE 10.8

A FULL CIRCULAR BUFFER

A circular buffer is empty when the in and out pointers are equal. It is full when the in pointer is one unit less than the out pointer. The code in Figure 10.9 implements a simple circular buffer.

```
#define NORMAL 0
#define EMPTY 1
#define FULL 2
#define BUFSZ 25

typedef struct buffer{
   int *bottom;              /* pointer to start of buffer */
   int *top;                 /* pointer to end of buffer   */
   int *in,*out;             /* pointers for in and out */
};

/* Test program for circular buffer routines. */

main()
{
   struct buffer userbuf;       /* define the buffer */
   int i,status,temp;
   char *malloc();

   /* The following code allocates space for the buffer and
      initializes all of the pointers */

   userbuf.in = userbuf.out = userbuf.bottom =
      malloc(sizeof(int)*BUFSZ);
   userbuf.top = userbuf.bottom + BUFSZ;

   /* The rest of the code just checks the buffer routines */

   for(i=1;i<20;i++){
      status = putbuf(&userbuf,i);
   }
   for(i=1;i<22;i++){              /* test normal and buffer empty */
      status = getbuf(&userbuf,&temp);
      printf("status = %d, data = %d\n",status,temp);
   }
   i=25;
   while(status != FULL){
      status = putbuf(&userbuf,i++);
   }
   while(status != EMPTY){
      status = getbuf(&userbuf,&temp);
      printf("status = %d, data = %d\n",status,temp);
   }
}
```

FIGURE 10.9 *(Part 1 of 2)*

```
/* Putbuf - place data into circular buffer
   Enter with pointer to buffer and data (int)

*/
putbuf(buf,data)
struct buffer *buf;
int data;
{
    int *temp;
    temp=buf->in;
    if(buf->in++ == buf->top)buf->in = buf->bottom;
    if(buf->in == buf->out){
        buf->in = temp;
        return(FULL);
    }
    else{
        *temp = data;
        printf("in %d out %d top %d bottom %d\n",
            buf->in,buf->out,buf->bottom,buf->top);
        return(NORMAL);
    }
}


/* getbuf - get data from circular buffer
   enter with pointer to buffer and pointer
   to integer data
*/

getbuf(buf,data)
struct buffer *buf;
int *data;
{
    if(buf->out == buf->in)return(EMPTY);
    *data=*buf->out;
    buf->out++;
    if(buf->out == buf->top)buf->out=buf->bottom;
    return(NORMAL);
}
```

FIGURE 10.9 *(Part 2 of 2)*

Note that the buffer handling routines work with a pointer to the buffer supplied by the calling function.

10.5 LINKED LISTS

Linked lists are an alternative to arrays with strong advantages under certain conditions. A linked list consists of a series of records in which each record contains a pointer to the next record.

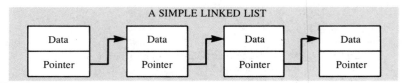

A SIMPLE LINKED LIST

FIGURE 10.10

The major disadvantage of linked lists is the increased storage required for the links. In C, this means increasing the storage for each record by one pointer variable. The major advantage is ease of insertion, deletion, searching, and sorting of records. The increase in storage requirements can be a major factor, but using linked lists allows the data to be placed in noncontiguous memory segments. An example of a linked list node definition is defined in Figure 10.11.

```
/*  definition of a node for a singly linked list */
struct node{
    char lastname[20];
    char firstname[10];
    struct node *next;
    };
```

FIGURE 10.11

This structure defines a node for a list of names. The pointer to the next node allows this to be used in a linked list.

Linked lists are easy to work with because only the links must be changed to insert or delete a record. This contrasts sharply with an array, where a portion of the array must be moved to perform an insertion or deletion. This advantage is critical in applications where large amounts of data are stored in memory and continously accessed and changed. For example, the function in Figure 10.12 on the opposite page, inserts a node.

```
/* Insert node in linked list.  Enter with pointers
    to node to insert and node to insert it after. */
void insertn(newnode,oldnode)
struct node *newnode *oldnode;
{
newnode->next=oldnode->next;
oldnode->next=newnode;
}
```

FIGURE 10.12

Notice that all that is required to insert the new node is changing two pointers.

One point to consider when using linked lists is that deleting records does not necessarily free up the memory used by that node. This brings about the problem of "garbage collection." Garbage collection is the process of collecting all of the disconnected, unused nodes into one usable chunk of memory. If programs operate for a long time inserting and deleting nodes of a linked list, garbage collection will become necessary.

One problem with singly-linked lists is encountered when deleting nodes. If you do not know the node that points to the current node, you cannot delete it, because deleting a node is merely replacing the pointer in the last node by the one in the node being deleted. One solution to this problem is shown in the doubly-linked list below.

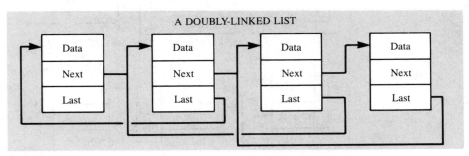

FIGURE 10.13

The doubly-linked list has the advantage of allowing two-directional travel. The list can be scanned forward or backward. Figure 10.14 shows the definition of a node for a doubly-linked list.

```
/*  definition of a node for a doubly linked list */
struct node{
    char lastname[20];
    char firstname[10];
    struct node *last;
    struct node *next;
    };
```

FIGURE 10.14

Let's look at what is required to swap to records in a doubly-linked list. This is the type of operation that must be performed in a bubble sort. To start with, we need the records to be swapped. We'll call them record A and record B. We also need the records previous to these records (C and D).

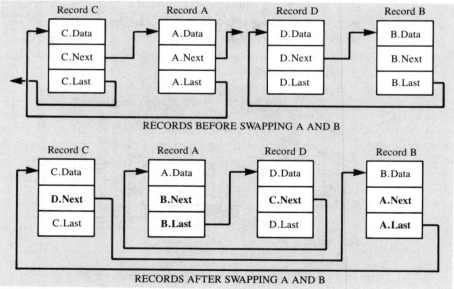

FIGURE 10.15

In Figure 10.15 on the previous page, all of the boldfaced variables are changed during the swap process. In general, dealing with linked lists is a very straightforward process, which is one of the reasons they are very common.

10.6 TREES

Trees are familiar data structures. Figure 10.16 is a drawing of a family tree.

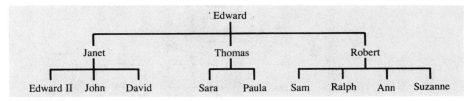

FIGURE 10.16

Trees can be used to describe any multilevel data structures where each element is itself a tree. Another common tree type is the bill of materials, which describes the pieces that go into constructing a product.

When describing data trees we call each branching point a node. The top-most node is called the root node, or simply the root. The standard representation of a tree is shown in Figure 10.18.

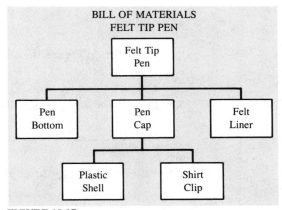

FIGURE 10.17

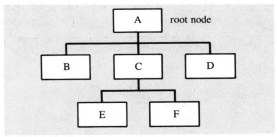

FIGURE 10.18

A tree is a set of one or more nodes, where one node is designated as the root node, and a set of subtrees are attached. Note that this is a recursive definition; i.e., a tree made up of trees.

There are many classes of trees, and often different ways of implementing the same tree type. One important type of tree is the binary tree. In binary trees each node has at most two daughters. A diagram of a binary tree is shown in Figure 10.19.

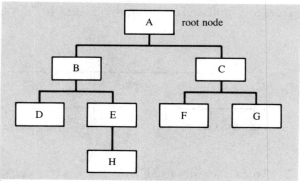

FIGURE 10.19

The tree in Figure 10.19 is relatively well-balanced, but that is not a requirement of trees.

The definition of a node structure for a tree which can have up to three daughters is shown in Figure 10.20 on the opposite page.

```
struct node{
    int data1;        /* Put the definition of the data here. */
         .
         .

    struct node *daughter1;    /* pointer to daughter 1 */
    struct node *daughter2;    /* pointer to daughter 2 */
    struct node *daughter3;    /* pointer to daughter 3 */
    }
```

FIGURE 10.20

Let's look at a definition of a tree node that will be used to define a tree representing the management structure of a company. The tree defined in Figure 10.21 can handle managers with up to ten people reporting to them.

```
struct node{
    char lastname[15];
    char firstname[15];
    char title[20];
    int grade;
    struct node *report[10];
    }
```

FIGURE 10.21

The definition of a binary tree is shown in Figure 10.22.

```
struct node{
    int data1;        /* Put the data definition here. */
        .
        .

    struct node *leftnode;     /* pointer to daughter 1 */
    struct node *rightnode;    /* pointer to daughter 2 */
    }
```

FIGURE 10.22

10.7 THE BINARY SEARCH TREE

Let's look in depth at one type of binary tree, the binary search tree. A binary search tree is used when the data can be sorted, and it is necessary to access the data quickly at a later point. Each node of the tree has two daughters and a rule for deciding on which side to look for an opening or to look for a value. The major advantage of search trees over sorted arrays is that no data needs to be moved to add data to the tree.

With a binary search tree, data is stored by checking the value of the data in each node against the value to be stored. At each occupied node, the left branch of the tree is taken if the value is less than the current node, and the right is taken if the value is greater than the node's value. This continues until an open node is found to store the data in.

Let's look at how a binary search tree would be built when passed a series of numbers. The storage/search rule is simple: numbers less than the value of a node are stored in the left branch; numbers greater are stored in the right branch. The first number encountered is used for the root node.

The series with which we will build the tree is:

5,3,4,8,2

The succession of trees produced as the numbers are added is shown in Figure 10.23.

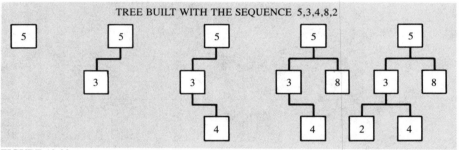

TREE BUILT WITH THE SEQUENCE 5,3,4,8,2

FIGURE 10.23

To search this tree for a value, we follow the same decision algorithm as we do when storing data. If we encounter a node without a link to follow down the tree, the search has failed. Otherwise, the program is to keep searching until the value is found.

For an example, we will look at a tree that is used to sort a series of numbers entered from the keyboard. The definition of this tree's nodes is shown in Figure 10.24 on the following page. The structure is defined as a **typedef** so that changes can be easily made to all routines.

```
typedef struct NODE{
      int data;
      struct node *left;
      struct node *right;
      };
#define TREESIZE 50
#define NUL 0
#include <stdio.h>
```

FIGURE 10.24

We have also defined the maximum size of the tree. The main routine for this program is very simple. The program will call function **fillbst** to input the data, function **prntasc** to print the numbers in ascending order, and function **prntdsc** to print the series in descending order. The program shown in Figure 10.25 allocates the space for the tree by declaring an array of nodes.

```
main()

{

   void fillbst(),displaybst(),prntasc(),prntdsc();
   struct NODE numbers[TREESIZE];

   fillbst(numbers);           /* fill the binary search tree */
   displaybst(numbers);        /* display the tree */
   prntasc(numbers);           /* print it in ascending order */
   prntdsc(numbers);           /* print it in descending order */

}
```

FIGURE 10.25

Function **fillbst**, which fills the tree, is shown in Figure 10.26 on the following page. This function calls function **getnumber** to ask the user for the data, and function **addnode** to add the data to the tree.

```
/*  fillbst is the function which loads the tree with data.
    Enter with a pointer to the tree. */

void fillbst(tree)
struct NODE tree[];
{
    int index = 0;
    int getnumber();
    int num;

    while((num=getnumber()) != -1){
        tree[index].data = num;
        tree[index].left = NUL;
        tree[index].right = NUL;
        if(index >0)addnode(tree,&tree[index]);
        index++;
        }
}


/* getnumber is a demo routine for inputting integers */

int getnumber()
{
    int num;
    printf("\n Enter a positive number, or -1 to end .");
    scanf("%d",&num);
    return(num);
}

/* addnode is a recursive routine to add nodes to a Binary
Search Tree where the left children are less than the parent
and the right children are equal or greater to the parent.

Enter with a pointer to the tree and a pointer to the
node to add */

addnode(tree,newnode)
struct NODE *tree,*newnode;
{
    if(newnode->data < tree->data){
        if(tree->left == NUL)tree->left = newnode;
        else addnode(tree->left,newnode);
        }
    else{
        if(tree->right == NUL)tree->right = newnode;
        else addnode(tree->right,newnode);
        }
}
```

FIGURE 10.26

The functions **prntasc** and **prntdsc** demonstrate traversal of the tree. The function **prntasc** demonstrates inorder traversal of the tree, and **prntdsc** demonstrates postorder traversal. These are both recursive functions, as shown in Figure 10.27.

```
void prntasc(tree)
struct NODE *tree;
{
    if(tree->left != NUL)prntasc(tree->left);
    printf("%d\n",tree->data);
    if(tree->right != NUL)prntasc(tree->right);

}

void prntdsc(tree)
struct NODE tree[];
{
    if(tree->right != NUL)prntdsc(tree->right);
    printf("%d\n",tree->data);
    if(tree->left != NUL)prntdsc(tree->left);

}
```

FIGURE 10.27

There are other types of trees, and other ways of building and accessing them, but this should give you the information needed to implement trees in C.

10.8 SUMMARY

When using any type of data structure, the first step is allocating memory. This can be done by declaring an array of the records to be used, or by dynamically allocating memory by requesting space from the operating system. The three C statements required for dynamic memory allocation are: **sizeof**, which returns the size of a variable; **malloc**, which requests memory from the system; and **free**, which releases memory back to the system.

Stacks are a very common type of data structure. They are commonly used for temporary data storage. The most significant feature of stacks is that the last item placed on the stack is the first one removed. This feature is commonly called last-in-first-out, or LIFO.

Linked lists are often used when an ordered list is being manipulated. The links make it very easy to insert or delete records from the list without moving large amounts of data, as would be necessary with arrays. A singly-linked list is used when the tree is always traversed in one direction. A doubly-linked list is used when the list must be traversed in both directions.

Many types of data are naturally represented by a tree data structure. A tree is a set of one or more nodes, where one node is designated the root node, and a set of subtrees are attached. The most commonly used type of tree is the binary tree. There are many types of tree data structures, and many ways of using them. If this chapter did not supply the information you need, consult a data-structures text.

REVIEW QUESTIONS

1. What is the difference between dynamic and standard memory allocation?
2. What are the advantages of dynamic memory allocation?
3. What problems may occur with dynamic memory allocation?
4. Is the statement

    ```
    int list[1000];
    ```

    an example of static or dynamic memory allocation?

5. For what purpose is the function **sizeof** used?
6. What data type is returned by **sizeof**?
7. Can a stack be split among multiple memory segments?
8. What are the meanings of the terms "push" and "pop" regarding stacks?
9. Are stacks an example of FIFO, or LIFO, storage?
10. What condition indicates that a stack is empty?
11. What condition indicates that a stack is full?
12. Are buffers an example of FIFO, or LIFO, storage?
13. What condition indicates that a circular buffer is empty?
14. What condition indicates when a circular buffer is full?
15. What is the major disadvantage of linked lists?
16. What is the major advantage of linked lists?
17. What is garbage collection?
18. What is a tree data structure?
19. Name three examples of data structures that can be easily represented with trees.
20. What is the root of a tree?

PROGRAMMING EXERCISES

1. Modify the circular buffer routines to work with lines of text terminated by the end-of-line marker ('\0'). The routine **putbuf** will have to be modified to work with a pointer to the data rather than the data itself. Make sure that the buffer-full condition works properly by notifying the calling routine if there is no room in the buffer for the passed string.

2. A "Reverse Polish Notation" (RPN) calculator uses a stack to hold intermediate results. To add the numbers $3+5$ together in RPN, you use the sequence:

   3 enter
   5 +

   and the calculator displays the result. Pressing the **enter** key places the displayed number on the stack. The sequence:

   3 enter
   4 enter
   5 +
   +

   will add 5 + 4 and then add 3, since the last operation acts on the displayed number and the top of the stack. Implement this calculator in C.

3. Create a function which will perform a bubble sort on a linked list. For this exercise the linked-list structure should contain a single integer for a data element.

4. Create a function to sort a double-linked list. Is the program simpler or more difficult than the function in Exercise 3?

5. Write a program to accept a series of numbers from the user, terminated by −1, and to build a binary sort tree from the data. The program should then enter search mode. In search mode the program will search the tree for numbers entered by the user, and notify the user if the number is in the tree.

PROGRAMMING PROJECT - STATISTICAL PROCESS CONTROL

A key to the success of Japanese manufacturing techniques has been the use of Statistical Process Control, or SPC. SPC is used to maintain consistent production by detecting variances outside of the statistical norm. The main tools used for this are the run chart and the frequency distribution. The goal of this project is to create a program to generate the charts used in SPC.

A run chart shows the change in data over time. This shows trends and patterns that might otherwise go undetected.

The frequency distribution is used to see if there is a skew to the data, and to see if the process is capable of producing parts within the required tolerances.

The program will be given the expected mean (M) and the expected variance (S). The operator will measure five parts each hour. These measurements will be entered into the computer. The program must plot each point and notify the operator if the average of the five parts is not within the range of M +/– 3∗S. In addition, the program must generate a report at the end of each day. To generate the report you need the following information:

1. The program must get the part number and the operation from the operator at the start of data gathering. This information should be printed at the top of every page of all reports.

2. The variance is calculated according to the following formula:

$$S = SQRT(((D_1 - M)^2 + (D_2 - M)^2 + \ldots (D_n - M)^2)/(n-1))$$

where S is the variance, D_1 is data 1 (in this case the first average), M is the mean, and n is the number of readings.

3. The program will print the run chart and a frequency distribution. In the run chart the data point is rounded to the nearest chart row, i.e., 12.529 is rounded to 12.520 in the example on the opposite page. In the frequency distribution the data is segregated in ranges. The data point 12.529 fits between 12.520 and 12.540.

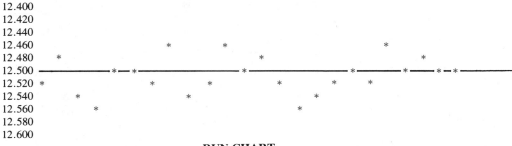

Part Number   345678   Operation 30 - Grind OD
Expected Mean   12.500   Expected Variation .020
Calculated Mean 12.510   Calculated Variation .027

```
12.400
12.420
12.440
12.460                       *           *                        *
12.480   *                                        *                        *
12.500 ——————————*—*——————————*———————————————*——————*——*—*——————
12.520 *               *           *           *         *       *
12.540      *                 *              *
12.560        *                                   *
12.580
12.600
```

RUN CHART

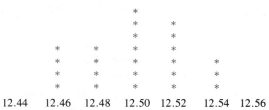

```
                          *
                          *       *
                          *       *
              *     *     *       *
              *     *     *       *     *
              *     *     *       *     *
              *     *     *       *     *
           12.44  12.46  12.48  12.50  12.52  12.54  12.56
```

FREQUENCY DISTRIBUTION

Measurements					*Average*
12.524	12.432	12.555	12.590	12.545	12.529
12.524	12.422	12.593	12.453	12.407	12.480
12.548	12.579	12.440	12.587	12.522	12.535
12.521	12.547	12.562	12.595	12.527	12.550
12.528	12.561	12.569	12.430	12.438	12.505
12.479	12.495	12.467	12.494	12.516	12.490
12.598	12.595	12.533	12.462	12.425	12.523
12.435	12.469	12.599	12.406	12.427	12.467
12.540	12.578	12.579	12.521	12.488	12.541
12.507	12.547	12.420	12.549	12.557	12.516
12.443	12.454	12.468	12.526	12.445	12.467
12.548	12.505	12.575	12.408	12.514	12.510
12.473	12.504	12.473	12.478	12.502	12.486
12.575	12.481	12.502	12.599	12.472	12.526
12.548	12.469	12.568	12.576	12.594	12.551
12.568	12.435	12.595	12.590	12.503	12.538
12.409	12.597	12.584	12.431	12.545	12.513
12.548	12.456	12.556	12.468	12.492	12.504
12.514	12.498	12.513	12.597	12.520	12.528
12.548	12.411	12.406	12.504	12.429	12.460
12.572	12.436	12.546	12.483	12.445	12.496
12.501	12.461	12.436	12.462	12.534	12.479
12.478	12.472	12.572	12.572	12.421	12.503
12.485	12.403	12.567	12.510	12.545	12.502

DATA

Programming Hints for This Project

1. Design your program structure carefully. The opening menu should look like:

Select from the following options.

A. Set up the program.
B. Acquire and screen data.
C. Print the run report.
X. Exit the program.

Enter your choice (A,B,C or X).

This implies three separate functions: **setup**, which gets the expected mean and variance; **run**, which gets the data from the user and checks if data is beyond limits (usually +/- 3S); and **report**, which prints the above report.

2. The data structure and data passing will be important issues. The crudest data handling would be to make all data external. A more structured approach would be to define a structure data type, using **typedef**, and pass a pointer to a structure of that type to each function that needs to access the data. This definition would look like:

```
typedef struct data{
    char partnum[12];               /* Part number */
    char operation[30];             /* Operation name */
    int mean;                       /* Expected mean */
    int var;                        /* Expected variation */
    float readings[30][5];          /* Data from operation */
}DATA,*DATAPTR;                     /* Type names */
```

These hints should help a little, but the program design and programming are up to you.

STANDARD
SYSTEM
FUNCTIONS

LEARNING OBJECTIVES

- Provide a reference for library functions.
- Introduce building your own function libraries.

Chapter

STANDARD
SYSTEM
FUNCTIONS

11.1 COMMON LIBRARY FUNCTIONS

The C language has no built-in capabilities to perform the basic functions required to produce useful programs. These requirements are usually met by function libraries supplied with the compiler. By consensus these functions have become standardized across compilers. The following section provides information on the most common functions.

These functions are the ones most commonly implemented with compilers, but you should check your compiler manual to see if these functions are implemented, and if the usage is the same as described here.

11.2 INPUT AND OUTPUT FUNCTIONS

All C compilers include the basic input and output routines. These routines require that the file **stdio.h** be included in the program.

11.3 FORMATTED INPUT AND OUTPUT

General Rules of Format Conversion

Conversion control strings can be embedded inside format specifiers, along with character data. A conversion control string is marked by a percent sign (%). For example, if used in a print statement, the format control string

"At the age of %d, %s weighed %d pounds."

specifies that a constant string will be printed with three variables. If the variables 3, "John", and 34 were passed to the function, the string

At the age of 3, John weighed 34 pounds.

would be printed.

The general format of a conversion control string is:

%[–][width][flags]conversion-code

where the parameters enclosed in brackets are optional.

%   — The percent sign marks the start of a conversion control string.
–   — The minus sign specifies that the data is to be printed left-justified.
width — All format strings can have a width specified. For example

%5d

specifies that an integer is to be printed five characters wide.
flags — Type-specific information. For example, this could specify the precision of a floating-point number.

Character Format Control

%s	Character string. The parameter must be a pointer to a string.
%c	Single character.

Integer Format Control

l	The letter l option specifies that the passed integer is of type long. This can be used with all integer format control specifics.
%d	Integer in decimal format.
%ld	Long integer in decimal format.
%u	Unsigned decimal.
%o	Octal.
%x	Hexadecimal.
%X	Hexadecimal using uppercase letters.

Floating-Point Format Control

%f	Floating-point number.
%e	Floating-point number in exponential format.
%g	Choose the shorter format between f and g.

The floating-point formats accept a width specifier for both sides of the decimal point, i.e. %3.2f will print three places to the left and two to the right of the decimal point.

11.4 THE FORMATTED I/O FUNCTIONS

printf —

The **printf** function is one of the most commonly used. It will print formatted data to **stdout**.

type	int
format	printf("format string"[,arg1,arg2,...,argn])

The format string is any string constant or variable. Additional arguments are included to match conversion control strings embedded in the format string.

EXAMPLE:

```
int temp,printf();
printf("Hello, the temperature is %d.",temp);

int printf();
float price;
printf("The sale price is $%1.2f",price);
```

The first example will print the integer value of **temp**. The second example will print a price, for example $1.25. Note that it will not print $23.45, since the format specifies only one character to the left of the decimal place. Be careful.

fprintf —

This if the same as **printf**, except that it accepts a file pointer argument. The file must have been previously opened in write or append mode.

type   int
format   fprintf(fp,"format string"[,arg1,arg2,...,argn])

fp is a file pointer assigned a value by the **fopen** function and the format string is any string constant or variable. Additional arguments are included to match conversion control strings embedded in the format string.

EXAMPLE:

```
FILE *fp;
int fprintf();
fp=fopen("data","w");
fprintf(fp,"Hello world.\n");
```

scanf —

This is the other side of formatted I/O. **Scanf** accepts the same arguments as **printf** with one very important difference. All of the data arguments must be pointers. The reason for this is clear if you remember that functions cannot directly change a passed variable.

type   int
format   scanf("format string"[,arg1,arg2,...,argn])

The format string is any string constant or variable. Additional arguments are included to match conversion control strings embedded in the format string. All additional arguments must be pointers. If characters other than conversion control strings are included in the format string, they must match the input stream. These characters are discarded.

EXAMPLE:

```
int temp,scanf();
scanf("%d",&temp);        /* Note the address operator. */
```

continued

```
int scanf();
float price;
scanf("%.2f",&price);

int scanf();
int age;
scanf("xxxx %2d",&age);   /* Discard junk and read age. */
```

fscanf —

This function reads formatted data from a file.

    type   int
    format   fscanf(fp,"format string"[,arg1,arg2,...,argn])

fp is a file pointer and the format string is any string constant or variable. Additional arguments are included to match conversion control strings embedded in the format string. All additional arguments must be pointers.

EXAMPLE:

```
int temp,fscanf();
fp=fopen("test","r");
fscanf(fp,"%d",&temp);     /* Note the address operator. */

int fscanf();
float price;
fp=fopen("test","r");
fscanf(fp,"%.2f",&price);
```

gets —

This function **gets** a string from **stdin**.

    type   int
    format   gets(string)

string is a pointer to a string buffer. This function reads characters into the buffer until a new line (\n) or the end of file is encountered.

EXAMPLE:

```
int x;
int gets();

char buffer[120];

x=gets(buffer);
```

puts —

The function **puts** writes a string to **stdout** and adds a new line.

type   int
format   x = puts(string)

The variable **x** is an integer and **string** is a pointer to a terminated string.

EXAMPLE:

```
int x;
int puts();

char *ch = "test string";

x=puts(ch);
```

fgets —

This function reads a string from a file. The function offers an argument for maximum size of the string being read. This is a useful error-trapping feature.

type   int
format   fgets(string,length,fp);

string is a pointer to a character string, **length** is an integer quantity specifying the maximum string length, and **fp** is a pointer to an open file.

EXAMPLE:

```
int x;
int fgets();
FILE *fp;
char buffer[120];

fp = fopen("test","r");

x = fgets(buffer,120,fp);
```

fputs —

This function writes a string to a file. The function offers an argument for maximum size of the string being read. This is a useful error-trapping feature.

type   int
format   x = fputs(string,fp);

x is an integer and **string** is a pointer to a character string and **fp** is a pointer to an open file. An error (−1) is returned if an error occurs writing the string.

EXAMPLE:

```
int x;
int fputs();
FILE *fp;
char *ch = "test string";
fp = fopen("test","w");

x = fputs(ch,fp);
```

putchar —

The **putchar** function writes a character to the terminal (if stdout was not redirected).

type   int
format   x = putchar(character);

x is an integer variable, and character is a variable or constant of type **char**. A value of −1 is returned if an error is encountered when writing the character. An error is usually encountered only when output has been redirected to an unopened file.

EXAMPLE:

```
char ch;
int x;

x = putchar(ch);
```

getchar —

The **getchar** function reads a character from the keyboard (if stdin has not been redirected).

type   int
format   x = getchar(character);

x is an integer variable, and **character** is a variable or constant of type **char**. A value of −1 is returned if an error is encountered when reading a character. An error is usually encountered only when input has been redirected to an unopened file.

EXAMPLE:

```
char ch;
int x;

x = getchar(ch);
```

11.5 STRING CONVERSION FUNCTIONS

sprintf —

The **sprintf** function performs the same format conversions that are available with **printf** and **fprintf**, but the resulting string is placed in memory rather than being printed.

type	int
format	fprintf(pointer,"format string"[,arg1,arg2,...,argn])

pointer is a string pointer to an open space large enough to contain the result of the format conversion. The format string is any string constant or variable. Additional arguments are included to match conversion control strings embedded in the format string.

EXAMPLE:

```
char result[30];
int sprintf();
sprintf(result,"Hello world.\n");
```

sscanf —

The **sscanf** function is used for in-memory format conversions. The most common use is for extracting data from a string of a known format.

type	int
format	sscanf(pointer,"format string"[,arg1,arg2,...,argn])

pointer is a pointer to a string and the format string is any string constant or variable. Additional arguments are included to match conversion control strings embedded in the format string. All additional arguments must be pointers.

EXAMPLE:

```
int sscanf();
float temp;
char string[30]="The price is $4.25";
sscanf(string,"The price is $%1.2f",&temp);
            /* note the address operator */
```

11.6 FILE ACCESS FUNCTIONS

File access requires that the file **stdio.h** be included at the beginning of the program. This include file contains the necessary declarations to define the data types and functions used in file I/O.

fopen —

The **fopen** function sets the necessary parameters for access to a file. This function must be called before a file can be read or written.

type   FILE *
format   fp = fopen("name","r")

where variable **fp** has previously been declared as type **FILE ***, **name** is a string constant or pointer to a legal file name, and **"r"** is a string containing a legal mode. The file mode determines what operations on the file are legal. A file opened as read-only cannot be written to. Legal types are

r   read only
w   write only
a   append

When a file is opened as read-only, it must exist. For write and append modes, a file will be created if it does not already exist.

Returned values:

NULL   fopen failed
file pointer   fopen succeeded

EXAMPLE:

```
#include <stdio.h>
main()
{
    FILE *fp;
    fp=fopen("datafile","r");
    if(fp == NULL){
        printf("An error occurred opening datafile.\n");
        exit();
        }

    char mode[4]="w";
    char filenam[20]="records";
    FILE *fpout;
    fpout=fopen(filenam,mode);
```

fclose —

The **fclose** function releases a file. All buffers associated with the file are flushed before the file is closed.

> type   int
> format   fclose(file pointer)

The file pointer must be initialized by **fopen**. Files are automatically closed when a program exits normally.

EXAMPLE:

```
fclose(fp);
```

fgetc —

fgetc gets one character from the specified file.

> type   char
> format   ch = fgetc(fp);

ch is a **char** type variable and **fp** is a file pointer initialized by **fopen**.

fputc —

fputc puts one character to the specified file.

> type   char
> format   stat = fputc(ch,fp);

ch is a **char** type variable, **stat** is an **int**, and **fp** is a file pointer initialized by **fopen**. The file must be opened in write or append mode.

Note that **putc** performs the same function as **fputc**, but is usually implemented as a macro rather than a function. This can cause unexpected effects in your program. Check this out carefully and use **putc** only if it is absolutely necessary.

getc —

getc gets one character from the specified file.

type   char
format   ch = getc(fp);

ch is a **char** type variable and **fp** is a file pointer initialized by **fopen**.

putc —

putc puts one character to the specified file.

type   char
format   stat = putc(ch,fp);

ch is a **char** type variable, **stat** is an **int**, and **fp** is a file pointer initialized by **fopen**. The file must be opened in write or append mode.

fgets —

This function reads the next line from the specified file. One advantage of using **fgets** is that you can specify a maximum length of input line.

type   int
format   stat = fgets(string,length,fp);

string is a pointer to a character array, **length** is an integer value specifying the maximum line length to read, and **fp** is a file pointer initialized by **fopen**.

EXAMPLE:

```
int stat,fgets();
char string[50];
FILE *fp;
fp=fopen("test","r");
stat=fgets(string,50,fp);
```

fputs —

The **fputs** writes a string to a file.

type   int
format   stat = fputs(string,fp);

stat is an integer. The value –1 will be returned if an error is encountered while writing. The variable **string** is a pointer to a properly terminated character array, and **fp** is a file pointer initialized by **fopen** in write or append mode.

EXAMPLE:

```
int stat,fputs();
char *string="This is a test";
FILE *fp;
fp=fopen("test","w");
stat=fputs(string,fp);
```

fread —

This function reads data from a file.

type   int
format   stat = fread(buffer,size,count,fp);

stat is an integer that will be assigned the number of items read, **buffer** is a pointer to the memory which will receive the data from the file, **size** is the size of the data types being read, **count** is the maximum number of those data types to read, and **fp** is a file pointer initialized by **fopen**.

EXAMPLE:

```
int stat,fread();
int array[100];
FILE *fp;
fp=fopen("data","r");
stat=fread(array,sizeof(int),100,fp);
printf("\n %d integers were read from file data.",stat);
```

fwrite —

This function writes data to a file.

type   int
format   stat = fread(buffer,size,count,fp);

stat is an integer that will be assigned the number of items written, **buffer** is a pointer to the memory which contains the data from the file,

size is the size of the data types being written, **count** is the number of those data types to be written, and **fp** is a file pointer initialized by **fopen** in write or append mode.

EXAMPLE:

```
int stat,fread();
int array[100];
FILE *fp;
        .
        .
        .         /* code which fills the array with data */

fp=fopen("data","w");
stat=fwrite(array,sizeof(int),100,fp);
```

freopen —

This function is used to reassign a file pointer that has been previously opened by **fopen**. This function can be used to redirect the streams stdin, stdout, and stderr.

type   int
format   fp = freopen("data","w",fp2);

fp is an uninitialized file pointer and **fp2** is a previously initialized stream.

EXAMPLE:

```
FILE *fp,*fp2;
fp=fopen("test","r");
fp2=freopen("test2","r",fp);
```

fflush —

This function is used to flush system buffers. This is used when writing a file to insure that no data is lost if the program is interrupted.

type   int
format   stat = fflush(fp);

stat is an integer variable, and **fp** is a file pointer initialized by **fopen** in write mode. A zero is returned if the file was successfully flushed.

EXAMPLE:

```
int stat,fflush();
FILE *fp;
fp=fopen("data","w");
stat=fflush(fp);
```

ftell —

This function returns the current file position. Used in conjunction with the **fseek** function, it provides a means of random file access.

    type   long
    format   position = ftell(fp);

The variable, **fp**, is a file pointer initialized by **fopen**.

EXAMPLE:

```
long pos;
FILE *fp;
fp=fopen("data","r");
       .
       .
       .
pos=ftell(fp);
```

fseek —

This function causes a file pointer to be repositioned to a location within a file. In conjunction with **ftell** it can be used to implement random file access.

    type   int
    format   stat = fseek(fp,position);

stat is an integer variable, **fp** is a file pointer initialized by **fopen**, and **position** is a long integer containing the offset from the beginning of the file in bytes to which to set the position. A −1 is returned if the seek fails.

EXAMPLE:

```
int stat;
FILE *fp;
long pos;
       .
       .
       .
pos=ftell(fp);
       .
       .
       .
stat=fseek(fp,pos);
```

rewind —

This function resets a file pointer to the beginning of a file.

> type   int
> format   stat = rewind(fp);

stat is an integer variable and **fp** is a file pointer initialized by **fopen**.

EXAMPLE:

```
int stat;
FILE *fp;
fp=fopen("data","r");
stat=rewind(fp);
```

11.7 STRING HANDLING FUNCTIONS

These functions are used for string manipulation and comparing. Note that there are implementation differences in these functions, usually in the returned values.

strcat —

This function concatenates strings.

> type   void
> format   strcat(string1,string2);

The variables **string1** and **string2** are pointers to properly terminated character arrays. After execution **string1** will contain the concatenated string. No error trapping is performed, so make sure the destination string is long enough to contain the concatenated string.

EXAMPLE:

```
char *string1 = "Hello";
char *string2 = " world.\n";
strcat(string1,string2);
    /* string1 is now "Hello world." */
```

strcmp —

The **strcmp** function compares two strings.

> type   int
> format   x = strcmp(string1,string2);

The variable **x** is an **int** variable and **string1** and **string2** are properly terminated strings. A zero is returned if the strings are equal; a positive number is returned if the first string is greater than the second; and a negative number is returned if it is less than the second. The returned value is determined by subtracting the first mismatched character of the second string from the corresponding character of the first.

EXAMPLE:

```
string1 = "ABCD"
string2 = "ABCE"
string3 = "ABCDE"
int x;
x = strcmp(string1,string2); /* will return a negative */
x = strcmp(string2,string1); /* will return a positive */
x = strcmp(string1,string1);  /* will return 0 */
x = strcmp(string1,string3); /* will return a negative */
```

strcpy —

The **strcpy** function copies strings. Note that the function does not check if the destination string is large enough to accept the string.

type   void
format   strcpy(string1,string2);

string1 is a properly terminated string and **string2** is a pointer to a space large enough (hopefully) to accept the string.

EXAMPLE:

```
char dest[20];          /* note this is big enough */
char *source = "CDEDF";

strcpy(source,dest);
```

contrast this with

```
char *dest;                   /* wrong wrong wrong */
char *source = "CDEDF";
strcpy(source,dest);          /* wrong wrong wrong */
```

where the string is copied to a pointer that is not pointing to an open buffer.

strlen —

The **strlen** function returns the length of a string.

    type   int
    format   x = strlen(string);

where **x** is a variable of type **int**, and **string** is a properly terminated string.

EXAMPLE:

```
string = "ABCDEFGHI"
int x;

x = strlen(string);      /* x will equal 9 */
```

The returned number is the number of characters not including the null byte that terminates the string.

11.8 CHARACTER CHECKING FUNCTIONS

These functions are implemented as macros rather than functions in most compilers.

isalpha —

The **isalpha** macro checks if the passed character is alphabetic. This functions returns a nonzero if the passed character is either an upper- or lower-case letter.

    type   This macro assigns an integer.
    format   x = isalpha(ch);

ch is a variable of type **char**.

EXAMPLE:

```
char ch;
int x;

x=isalpha(ch);
```

isupper —

The **isupper** macro checks if the argument is an uppercase letter. The macro returns a nonzero if it is, and a zero if it is not.

    type   This macro returns an integer value.

    format   x = isupper(ch);

ch is of type **char** and **x** is an **integer**.

islower —

The **islower** macro checks if the argument is a lowercase letter. The macro returns a nonzero if it is, and a zero if it is not.

    type   This macro returns an integer value.

    format   x = islower(ch);

ch is of type **char** and **x** is an **integer**.

isdigit —

The **isdigit** macro checks if the argument is a number. The macro returns a nonzero if it is, and a zero if it is not.

    type   This macro returns an integer value.

    format   x = isnumber(ch);

ch is of type **char** and **x** is an **integer**.

isalnum —

isalnum checks if the argument is numeric or alphabetic. The macro returns a nonzero if it is, and a zero if the character is neither a letter nor a number.

    type   This macro returns an integer value.

    format   x = isalnum(ch);

ch is of type **char** and **x** is an **integer**.

isascii —

This function returns a nonzero if the argument is a legal ASCII character. The legal characters are the decimal values 0–127.

type   This macro returns an integer value.
format   x = isascii(ch);

ch is of type **char** and **x** is an **integer**.

11.9 MEMORY ALLOCATION FUNCTIONS

sizeof —

The **sizeof** function returns the size of a variable or a data type in bytes.

type   int
format   size = sizeof(float);
            size = sizeof(temperature);

The first example will assign the size of the **float** data type to the variable **size**. The second example will assign the size of the variable **temperature** to the variable **size**. This can be used to return the size of structures.

EXAMPLE:

```
int x,sizeof();
x=sizeof(float);

struct car{
     int year;
     char name[20];
     }test;
int x,sizeof();
x=sizeof(test);
```

malloc —

malloc is used to ask the operating system for a block of memory for data.

type   *char;
format   pointer = malloc(numbytes);

pointer is a pointer which will be assigned the address of a block of memory **numbytes** long. Combined with the **sizeof** function, **malloc** can be used to allocate memory an array of any variable type.

EXAMPLE:

```
char *malloc();
char *memory;
memory = malloc(1000);

char *malloc()
char *memory;
int requirement;
requirement = sizeof(float)*1000;
memory = malloc(requirement);
```

free —

The **free** function releases memory previously allocated by the **malloc** function.

type   int
format   free(pointer);

The variable **pointer** must have been previously assigned by **malloc** to point to a block of memory.

EXAMPLE:

```
char *memory, *malloc();
memory=malloc(1000)        /* Allocate 1000 locations. */
free(memory);              /* Give memory back to system. */
```

11.10 MISCELLANEOUS FUNCTIONS

qsort —

The **qsort** function is used to sort an array using the quick-sort algorithm developed by C. A. R. Hoare. To use this function you must supply a function to compare two elements of the array.

type   void
format   qsort(array,elements,size,compare);

array is a pointer to the array to sort, **elements** is the number of elements to sort, **size** is the size in bytes of each element, and **compare** is a pointer to a function which compares two elements of the array. The **compare** function, of type int, accepts two pointers to elements of the array and returns:

-1   if argument1 < argument2
0   if argument1 = = argument2
1   if argument1 > argument2

EXAMPLE:

```
int   array[100];
int   compare();
        .
        .
        .
qsort(array,100,sizeof(int),&compare());

compare(p1,p2)
int *p1,*p2;
{
    if(*p1<*p2)return(-1);
    if(*p1==*p2)return(0);
    return(1);
}
```

rand —

This function returns a random number. In some compilers this function returns a random integer; in others it returns a random floating point number. Check your compiler for specifics about this function.

11.11 BUILDING YOUR OWN FUNCTION LIBRARIES

The use of function libraries allows C programmers to develop large, complex programs in a structured manner that promotes ease of maintenance and modification. Most compilers come with standard function libraries for system-related and math functions. Functions more closely related to a particular application must be developed or purchased separately.

In developing function libraries for applications, start by grouping the functions. The groupings should be by functional area rather than by operational level. For example, a database program may require a large number of functions dealing with the maintenance of the database ranging from those that read and write records up through the sorting and searching functions. The same program may also have a group of functions that deal with the user interface including various levels of display routines.

If the functions in a library are clearly defined, with each function performing one task, there will be a few "high-level" functions and many "low-level" functions. Let's look at the makeup of a function library which handles the screen display for a commercial program.

Top Level	
display	update screen based on current situation. This function uses many second level functions.
Second Level	
dspsttus	display current status
dspmenu	display current menu choices
border	draw the screen border
clrscrn	clear the screen
Third Level	
box	draw a colored box
line	draw a line of selected color
clrline	clear a line of text
Bottom Level	
curpos	position cursor
setborder	set the screen border color
cprintf	formatted print with color options
cputchar	print one character with color options
stattrib	set a screen character's attributes

In the UNIX environment the **ar** program is used to create program libraries from object files. These archive libraries can then be processed with **ranlib** to produce libraries usable by the loader.

11.12 SUMMARY

Most C compilers supply function libraries with functions for interfacing with the system and performing common utility tasks. All C compilers include the basic input and output routines. These routines require that the file **stdio.h** be included in the program. The functions use the following format control strings.

Character Format Control

%s	Character string. The parameter must be a pointer to a string.
%c	Single character.

Integer Format Control

l	The letter l option specifies that the passed integer is of type long. This can be used with all integer format control specifics.
%d	Integer in decimal format.
%ld	Long integer in decimal format.
%u	Unsigned decimal.
%o	Octal.
%x	Hexadecimal.
%X	Hexadecimal using uppercase letters.

Floating-Point Format Control

%f	Floating-point number.
%e	Floating-point number in exponential format.
%g	Choose the shorter format between f and g.

Formatted I/O Functions

printf — The **printf** function prints formatted data to **stdout**.

fprintf — This if the same as **printf**, except that it accepts a file pointer argument.

scanf — The **scanf** reads formatted data from **stdin**.

fscanf — This function reads formatted data from a file.

gets — This function **gets** a string from **stdin**.

puts — The function **puts** writes a string to **stdout** and adds a new line.

fgets — This function reads a string from a file.

fputs — This function writes a string to a file.

putchar — The **putchar** function writes a character to the terminal (if stdout was not redirected).

getchar — The **getchar** function reads a character from the keyboard (if stdin has not been redirected).

String Conversion Functions

sprintf — The **sprintf** function performs the same format conversions that are available with **printf** and **fprintf**, but the resulting string is placed in memory rather than being printed.

sscanf — The **sscanf** function is used for in-memory format conversions.

File Access Functions

fopen — The **fopen** function sets the necessary parameters for access to a file. This function must be called before a file can be read or written.

fclose — The **fclose** function releases a file.

fgetc — **fgetc** gets one character from the specified file.

fputc — **fputc** puts one character in the specified file.

getc — **getc** gets one character from the specified file.

putc — **putc** puts one character to the specified file.

fgets — This function reads the next line from the specified file.

fputs — The **fputs** writes a string to a file.

fread — This function reads data from a file.

fwrite — This function writes data to a file.

freopen — This function is used to reassign a file pointer that has been previously opened by **fopen**.

fflush — This function is used to flush system buffers.

ftell — This function returns the current file position.

fseek — This function causes a file pointer to be repositioned to a location within a file.

rewind — This function resets a file pointer to the beginning of a file.

String Handling Functions

strcat — This function concatenates strings.

strcmp — The **strcmp** function compares two strings.

strcpy — The **strcpy** function copies strings.

strlen — The **strlen** function returns the length of a string.

Character Checking Functions

isalpha — The **isalpha** macro checks if the passed character is alphabetic.

isupper — The **isupper** macro checks if the argument is an uppercase letter.

islower — The **islower** macro checks if the argument is a lowercase letter.

isdigit — The **isdigit** macro checks if the argument is a number.

isalnum — **isalnum** checks if the argument is numeric or alphabetic.

isascii — This function returns a nonzero if the argument is a legal ASCII character.

Memory Allocation Functions

sizeof — The **sizeof** function returns the size in bytes of a variable or a data type.

malloc — **malloc** is used to ask the operating system for a block of memory for data.

free — The **free** function releases memory previously allocated by the **malloc** function.

Miscellaneous Functions

qsort — The **qsort** function is used to sort an array using the quick-sort algorithm.

rand — This function returns a random number.

REVIEW QUESTIONS

1. Which of the following **printf** statements contain errors?
   a. printf("This is a good line.");
   b. printf("Charlie said, "This is a good line"".");
   c. printf("Donna said, \"This is a good line.\"");
   d. printf("There are %d cars in the system.",&cars);
   e. printf("Change your directory to \%d.",dirnum);
   f. printf("%d\% of the cars are missing.",miscars);
   g. printf("The cost is $1.2d.",cost);
   h. printf("The company spent $%d% of its income.");
2. What is the difference between **putc** and **fputc**?
3. Given the declarations

   int number;
   float temperature;
   char string[20];

   which of the following **scanf** statements contain errors?
   a. scanf("%s %d",string,number);
   b. scanf("%s, %d,string,number);
   c. scanf("%s%d",string,number);
   d. scanf("%s %d",&string,number);
   e. scanf("%s,%d",&string[1],&number);

f. scanf("%4.6f",temperature);
g. scanf("%4.6",&temperature);
h. scanf("%4.6f",&temperature);

4. What are the legal values with your compiler for the mode in which a file can be opened?
5. What value does the compiler return when a file cannot be opened?
6. What data type is returned from the **fopen** function?
7. Is the **fclose** function needed before an **exit**?
8. What two functions can be used instead of the **freopen** function to reassign a file pointer from one file to another?
9. What is the difference between the **strcpy** and the **strcat** function?
10. What values are returned by the **rand** function on your system?
11. What function type must be provided to compare values for the **qsort** function?
12. How can the **freopen** function be used to redirect output from a program?
13. What is the range of values checked for by the following functions? (For example, **isdigit** checks for characters 0–9.)
a. isalpha
b. isupper
c. islower
d. isalnum
e. isascii
14. What is the final value of the variable **length** in the following code segment?

```
int length;
char *string = "ABC";
length = strlen(string);
```

15. What type is the function **ftell**?
16. What argument type is passed to the function **fseek**?
17. What type is the function **malloc**?
18. What is the purpose of the function **free**?
19. One of the arguments to the function **qsort** is a function. What is its purpose?
20. What is the range of values returned by the **rand** function on your system?

PROGRAMMING EXERCISES

1. Enter and run the following program on your system. The results will tell you the values returned by the string compare function.

```
main()
{
    char *string1 = "ABC";
    char *string2 = "ABD";
    char *string3 = "ABCD";
    int result;

    result=strcmp(string1,string1);
    printf("\nstrcmp returns %d when the strings are equal.\n",result);
    result=strcmp(string1,string2);
    printf("\nstrcmp returns %d when string2 > string1.\n",result);
    result=strcmp(string2,string1);
    printf("\nstrcmp returns %d when string2 < string1.\n",result);
    result=strcmp(string1,string3);
    printf("\nstrcmp returns %d when string2 is longer than string1.\n",
        result);
}
```

2. Enter and debug the following program.

```
#include <stdio>
main()
{
int i;
FILE fp;

fp=fopen("test",r);
for(i=0;i=10;i++){
     fprintf("%d decimal = %h hex = %o octal",i,i,i);
     }
fp = fclose();
}
```

3. Write a program that will read a file and check the spelling of each word in the file against words contained in another file, which is named **library**. A word is defined as a collection of letters surrounded by spaces or punctuation. Any words that are not included in the library file should be printed on the screen. The program can assume that any non-ASCII character is a terminator. The compares should ignore case. The program should operate on a sorted library file. There is no need to develop a special format for the library file.

   Note that if the string compare function is to be used, the words will have to be properly terminated before the call to **strcmp**.

4. Write a program to sort arrays of structures using the **qsort** function. The structure should include the following information:

   a. Last name
   b. First name
   c. Middle initial
   d. Street address
   e. Town
   f. State
   g. Zip code
   h. Group code

   The program should allow sorts based on last names, zip codes, and group codes.

5. Write a program to test the quality of random numbers generated by your system. Draw a graph of 10,000 numbers and the distribution of these numbers within 10 equal ranges that cover the legal range of numbers produced. If the random number generator is good, the distribution will be close to even among the groups.

PROGRAMMING PROJECT — SUPER COPY PROGRAM

We wish to create a copy program which has a few special features. These include:

1. Filtering the file and removing any non-ASCII characters. This is a commonly needed option when accessing files produced on another system, or produced by a program that did not intend the file to be read.
2. Filtering for upper- and lowercase characters. The program should offer the option of changing all lowercase characters to uppercase, changing all lowercase to uppercase, or looking for any uppercase characters that are not at the beginning of a sentence and displaying them. In the last instance the user should be prompted for each incidence.
3. Searching a file for a designated string. The program should offer a count option or a display option. The count option will merely count the number of occurrences; the display option will display each occurrence.
4. Statistics — The program should display the starting size and ending size, the number of words, and the number of lines in both files.

The program should accept the file names and the option on the command line, or, if the parameters are not supplied, provide full menu support.

DEBUGGING HINTS

LEARNING OBJECTIVES

- Offer a simple outline for debugging a program.
- Present a list of common errors.
- Provide exercises with common errors.

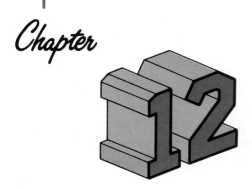

Chapter

DEBUGGING
HINTS

12.1 DEBUGGING

It often takes more time to debug a program than it does to design and initially code it. Of course, debugging is greatly simplified by good design and coding. Good debugging is a matter of strategy and tactics, not memorization of facts. Take time to consider debugging problems.

The first rule of debugging is to solve one problem at a time and build a secure base to work from. Once the secure base is established, defend it. Check the function of the secure areas after each addition to the code. Allowing a large body of code to become corrupted and not catching it early is the surest way to create a debugging nightmare. If the problem is detected when it is introduced, the problem of locating it is greatly simplified. A simple guideline for debugging follows:

Clean up the compile errors — This is an obvious and necessary step. Not only should fatal errors be fixed, but all warning messages also should be carefully checked and remedied, if possible.

Verify the basics — At the earliest possible time, test the basic assumptions upon which the program is based. If they are wrong, the program will usually require major changes. For example, if a database program requires random access to a certain file type, check the file positioning function as soon as possible, because if you can't make it work the program needs redesign.

Narrow the problem — Eliminate as many factors as possible. Determine when in the program flow the problem was introduced. If you are not using a debugger, place print statements in the program to tell you where the program went astray. The print statements should display the contents of any questionable variables. If your system buffers print statements, you may need to flush the buffer after each print, or to set the buffer size to zero before running the program.

Invest in diagnostics — Write functions that verify a set of conditions. Use the function to find where problems are introduced. If a program is large, it is often worth writing an exerciser program which will run the program under development and check for errors. This also offers a method of quickly checking the effect of program changes. The exerciser may be as simple as a file containing the program's input or a batch file containing commands.

Test exhaustively — When you are convinced the program is complete, test some more. Chart all possible program paths, and follow all of them. Check every data entry for error trapping. It is also a good idea to ask another person to help test the program.

Note: Remember to remove debugging code when the program goes into production. No user wants to see cryptic messages that are understandable only to the program's author.

12.2 COMMON ERRORS

There is an enormous number of problem types that can be introduced into a program, but some common classes cause a large portion of the problems.

System calls — In the early debugging phases, especially if your program disappears, look at your calls to I/O functions. Carefully check each access to new files, and each call to a different I/O function.

Mistyped operators — This is an insidious problem type because the statement often looks correct, even when examined carefully. For example the problem in

```
if(color = YELLOW)
```

is relatively easy to spot, but in a more complex line, such as

```
if((x1<y7)¦¦(x2>y6&&(x4<y4+y5))¦(x3==y3))
```

the problem is slightly harder to spot.

Operator logic errors — When dealing with complex statements it is common to have embedded logic errors. For example, the statement

```
x = (x6 * 3 * (y2+y3) + y1 * y2 + y3 / y1)
```

is different from

```
x = (x6 * 3 * (y2+y3) + (y1 * y2 + y3) / y1)
```

When in doubt, separate with parentheses, or break the statement into smaller units that are more easily understood and debugged.

Unassigned pointers — When data is stored using a pointer that has not been initialized, something will be messed up. The actual effects of such an action may be immediately apparent, or they may not become evident until much later, and sometimes the error is not discovered at all.

Overrun storage buffers — The other type of error encountered when using pointers occurs when data is stored beyond the end of buffers. For example:

```
int x[20];
int *px;

px = &x[0];

px += 21;

*px = 0;
```

is a roundabout way of storing a zero into the variable in memory just after the array **x**. Sequences such as the one above are common in many programs, but more spread out. Make sure you stay within your storage bounds. This sort of problem is most common in functions which receive a pointer as an argument and store data using that argument.

Data type errors — In some languages, such as Pascal, the typing is strongly enforced. In C, the typing is not strongly enforced and problems sometimes result. It is good policy to always explicitly coerce any data type changes. When problems start to arise, especially when the problem consists of wrong answers at the end of calculations, inspect every instance of data type change.

Mismatched function arguments — A common error is caused by not properly aligning arguments with function expectation. One way this can happen is during modifications. For example:

```
printf("The cost of %s is %d.",item,price);
```

might be modified to print to a file by changing **printf** to **fprintf**.

```
fprintf("The cost of %s is %d.",item,price); /* wrong */
```

The problem, of course, is that **fprintf** expects a file pointer. The correct statement would look like

```
fprintf(fp,"The cost of %s is %d.",item,price);
```

Without the file pointer, the program would likely hang. This is the type of error that can be hard to find, since no visible symptoms are produced by the error.

12.3 CONCLUSION

Debugging is often called more art than science because of the complexity of the problem and the large part intuition plays in the process, but the systematic approach to debugging is usually the more successful. With large programs made up of major modules, it is best to have a debugging plan as part of the overall development plan. By integrating the debugging with the code development, you will find the job of final debugging much simpler.

Finally, debugging is one of those things where practice improves your abilities. Design and debug as many of the exercises in this book as possible, or develop independent programs. The practice will hold you in good stead when major programs are to be developed.

12.4 SUMMARY

A simple outline for debugging follows:

1. Clean up the compile errors.
2. Verify the basics.
3. Narrow down the problem.
4. Invest in diagnostics.
5. Test exhaustively.

Some of the problem areas and common errors to look for are:

1. System calls.
2. Mistyped operators.
3. Operator logic errors.
4. Unassigned pointers.
5. Overrun storage buffers.
6. Data type errors.
7. Mismatched function arguments.

When debugging large programs have a debugging plan as part of the overall development plan; integrating the debugging with the code development will make the debugging much simpler.

PROGRAMMING EXERCISES

1. Enter the following program and debug it. There are numerous errors in the program. Correct the formatting first to make the operation more obvious.

```
main()
{
    char *string1 = "ABC;
    char *string2 = "ABD";
    char *string3 = "ABCD";
    int result;
```

continued

```
result = strcmp(string1,string1);
string3[5]='Q';
if(result = 0)
printf("\nstrcmp returns 0 when the strings are equal.\n");
else
printf("\strcmp returns nonzero when equal');
result=strcmp(strng1,strng2);
if(result<0)
printf("\nstrcmp returns %d when string2 > string1.\n",result);
result=strcmp(string2,string1);
prntf("\nstrcmp returns %d when string2 < string1.\n",result);
result==strcmp(string1,string3);
printf("\nstrcmp returns %d when string2 is longer
        than string1.\n",result);
}
```

2. The following program prints a graph of the height of a bouncing ball.

```
main()
{
    int height,vel=0,damping=2;
    int acc=-1;

    printf("Enter the interger starting height. ");
    scanf("%d",&height);
    while(height>0 || vel !=0){
        /* as long as we are not at rest */
        printit(height);
        height=height+vel;
        vel+=acc;
        if(height<=0){
            vel=(-damping)-vel;
            if(vel<0)vel=0;
            height=0;
        }
    }
}
printit(hgt)
int hgt;
{
    int x;
    for(x=1;x<hgt;x++)printf(" ");
    printf("X\n");
}
```

This version of the program does the same thing with one minor difference:

```
main()
{
    int height,vel=0,damping=2;
    int acc=-1;

    printf("Enter the interger starting height. ");
    scanf("%d",&height);
    while(height>0 || vel !=0){
        /* as long as we are not at rest */
        printit(height);
        height=height+vel;
        if(height<=0){
            vel=(-damping)-vel;
            if(vel<0)vel=0;
            height=0;
        }
        vel+=acc;

    }
}
printit(hgt)
int hgt;
{
    int x;
    for(x=1;x<hgt;x++)printf(" ");
    printf("X\n");
}
```

Enter the two programs, run them, and explain what effect the difference makes and why. The problem illustrated in this example is common. State the general condition and the means of avoiding the problem. Describe the symptoms that indicate this type of problem.

3. Enter and run the following program on your system.

```
main()
{
    float x,y;
    int z;
        x = 2.2;              /* 2.2 */
        printf("\nx = %1.1f\n",x);
        y = x + 1;            /* 3.2 */
        printf("\ny = %1.1f\n",y);
        y = x/1;                /* 2.2 or 2.0 if truncated */
        printf("\ny = %1.1f\n",y);
        z = y;                 /* 2 if true integer */
        printf("\nz = %1.1f - float",z);
        printf("\nz = %d - int\n",z);
        z = y + 2;             /* 5 if true integer */
        printf("\nz = %1.1f - float",z);
        printf("\nz = %d - int\n",z);
        x = z * 2;            /* 10 or 10.4 */
        printf("\nx = %1.1f\n",x);
        }
```

The results of this program are very compiler-dependent.

4. Enter and debug the following program. The intended results should be obvious.

```
/*
    This program contains errors.
*/

main()
{
    int array[1];
    int i;
    int sum;
    int getnumber();

    printf("\nEnter your numbers, one at a time.\n");
    printf("\nEnter -1 when done.\n");
    while(array[i++]=getnumber() >0){
        sum += array[i];
        if(i>20)break;
        }
    printf("\nThe Sum of the %d numbers is %d.",i,sum);
    printf("\nThe Average of the array is %d",sum/i);
    }
```

continued

```
/* getnumber is a demo routine for inputting integers */
int getnumber()
{
    int num;
    printf("\nEnter a positive number, or -1 to end .");
    scanf("%d",&num);
    return(num);
    }
```

5. Enter and correct the following program. The program should print the minimum of two numbers.

```
main()
{
    float i,j;    i = getnumber);    j = getnumber();
    i=min(i,j);
    printf("min = %d\n",i);
    }
min(num1,num2)
int num1,num2;
{
    return((num1<num2)?num1:num2);
    }
```

6. Change the following program to handle file open errors.

```
#include <stdio.h>       /* stdio.h contains equates for file
I/O */

main()
{
    char ch;
    FILE *source;
    FILE *destination;
    char srcename[20];
    char destname[20];

    printf("\nEnter the source file name.  ");
    scanf("%s",srcename);
    printf("\nEnter the destination file name.  ");
    scanf("%s",destname);
    source=fopen(srcename,"r");
    destination=fopen(destname,"w");

    while((ch=fgetc(source)) != EOF)fputc(ch,destination);
    exit();
    }
```

7. The following program is poorly structured and contains logical errors. Enter and debug it.

```c
#include <stdio.h>
/* This program contains errors.
   Do not emulate the coding style of this program
*/
/*  This program creates a random array, sorts it, and
    prints it to file temp */
main()

{
    int i,j;
    float data[25],avg;
    FILE *fp;
    fp=fopen("temp","w");
        fprintf(fp,"\n");
    for(j=0;j<25;j++){
        data[j]=12.4+((rand()%200)/1000.0);
        avg=avg+data[j];
    }
    for(i=0;i<25;i++){
        bsort(data,24);
        fprintf(fp,"%d\n",data[i]);
    }
}

bsort(array,length)        /* sort in ascending order */
int array[];
int length;
{
    int i,j;
    for(i=0;i<length-1;i++){
        for(j=i+1;j<length;j++){
            if(array[i] > array[j])swap(&array[i],&array[j]);
            }
        }
}
swap(a,b)
int a,b;
{
    int temp;
    temp = *a;
    *a=*b;
    *b=temp;
}
```

8. Enter and test the following test program. Describe the error and correct it. Why might this type of error go undetected if each module of a program is not tested exhaustively?

```
main()
{
    int card[52];
    int i;

    for(i=1;i<=52;i++)card[i]=i;
    shuffle(card,52);
    for(i=1;i<=52;i++)printf("Card %d = %d.\n",i,card[i]);
    }

/* shuffle - shuffle an array */
shuffle(array,n)
int array[];
int n;
{
    int temp;
    int i,x,y;

    for(y=1;y<4;y++){
    for(i=1;i<=n;i++){
        x=rand()%52;
        temp = array[x];
        array[x]=array[i];
        array[i]=temp;
        }
    }
    }
```

9. The following program contains a common type of error, confusing the use of pointers and ordinary variables. The program should create a random array of 20 integers, sort it and print it out in order. Make it work. Very few changes are required to fix it.

```
/* main program tests qsort function */
main()
{
    int sarray[20];
    int i;
    for(i=19;i>=0;i--)sarray[i]=i;
    qsort(sarray,20);
    for(i=0;i<20;i++)printf("%d\n",sarray[i]);
}
```

continued

```
/*  qsort - perform quick sort on an integer array.
    Enter with pointer to array and array lenght(int).
*/
qsort(array,length)        /* sort in ascending order */
int *array;
int length;
{
    int tophalf;
    int pivot;
    if(length>1){
        pivot=((*array+*(array+length-1))/2);
        tophalf=split(array,array+length-1,pivot);
        qsort(array,tophalf-array);
        qsort(tophalf,length-(tophalf-array));
    }
}


split(lowptr,highptr,pivot)
int *lowptr,*highptr;
int pivot;
{
    int temp;
    while(lowptr<=highptr){
        while(*lowptr<pivot)lowptr++;
        while(*highptr>pivot)highptr--;
        if(lowptr<=highptr){
            temp = *lowptr;
            *lowptr=*highptr;
            *highptr=temp;
            lowptr++;
            highptr--;
        }
    }
    return(lowptr);
}
```

10. The following copy program accepts arguments from the command line. The program may not work on your system. Check each step in the program and correct any errors.

```
/* To run this program type

      testcp source,destination

   The source file must exist.
*/
#include <stdio.h>

main(argc,argv)
int argc;
char **argv;
{
    FILE *infile,*outfile;
    char buffer[80];
    int i;
    int ch;


    /* The following line is a debugging aid - delete it
       when the program is working */
    for(i=0;i<=argc;i++)printf("arg %d = %s \n",i,argv[i]);


    if(argc != 2){
       printf("\nYou must provide two filenames.\n");
       exit();
       }
    infile=fopen(argv[1],"r");
    if(infile==NUL)[
       printf("\nFile %s could not be opened.\n",argv[1]);
       exit();
       }
    outfile=fopen(argv[2],"w");
    while((ch=fgetc(infile)) != EOF){
       fputc(ch,outfile);
       }
    printf("\nCopy complete.\n");
    }
```

EFFICIENCY
AND SPEED

LEARNING OBJECTIVES

- Introduce basics of program optimization.
- Discuss means of reducing memory requirements.
- Discuss techniques of increasing execution speed.

Chapter

EFFICIENCY
AND SPEED

13.1 PROGRAM OPTIMIZATION

Programming is a task of managing trade-offs. When the speed or memory requirements of a program become severe, trade-offs become more difficult. Before evaluating trade-offs, you should understand what the options are, and what the costs and benefits are of each of the options.

Before starting to analyze the possible ways of making your program faster or smaller, look at the program and ask a few basic questions. Is the program designed efficiently? Is the code well-structured and clean? Is the algorithm used the most efficient, or just the easiest to program? Once all of these questions are answered you can start looking for the extra bit of speed or memory savings. Lastly, make sure the program works correctly before starting to optimize it. Getting the wrong result more quickly is of little use.

13.2 OPTIMIZING COMPILERS

When there are speed and memory constraints, the first place to look for program improvements is the compiler. Many C compilers, including most UNIX compilers, offer an extra pass which optimizes code by removing redundancies and performing various levels of low-level restructuring for efficiency. The optimizing pass is activated with the **–o** option on most UNIX C compilers.

13.3 MEMORY CONSIDERATIONS

When memory requirements are important it is incumbent on the programmer to consider the variable memory requirements of different programming techniques.

Clean up any inefficiencies in the program — Check through the program for poorly written code, arrays larger than necessary, redundant strings, and the like. Cleaning up your program will often bring large returns in space usage.

Search for blocks of common code — The next step is to review the structure of the program to see if it can be condensed. Are there multiple areas that perform the same task? If so, maybe a function can perform the task more efficiently.

Let's consider the different memory use of macros and functions. The following function returns the minimum of two integers

```
min(num1,num2)
int num1,num2;
{
    return((num1<num2)?num1:num2);
    }
```

and the macro definition

```
#define min(num1,num2) ((num1<num2)?num1:num2)
```

does the same thing. However, the macro does the task in less space and uses less processing time. This is a slanted example, because the actual processing for the macro is less than the processing inside the function. The macro is still clearly more efficient as long as the total code inside the macro is less than the overhead caused by the function call. This can be determined by comparing the size of a macro call to the space required to add a function call. In addition, the function itself carries overhead. The amount of data needed for a function's overhead can be determined by placing the code in-line and comparing it with the space required when it is contained in a function.

In order to minimize the program's size, you need to know the break-even points of using functions. Once these points are known, the decision is simple: follow the path of least memory. But remember, not using functions will often make the program less understandable, harder to maintain, and less portable.

Utilize register variables — Use the C register variables to decrease the memory used for variable loading and storage. In most machines, using register variables saves the code space used to load a variable into a register before an operation and store it after the operation.

Use small data types — Use the smallest data type which will perform the function. In some cases using **unsigned** short integers can save the requirement of using a **long** variable.

Data type conversion — In some cases it is possible to translate an array of a certain variable type into a simpler type. For example, if the range of an array is between 3.100 and 3.335, the data can be stored as short integers with a range of 0 to 235 (or 100 — 335) and a conversion performed when the data is stored and retrieved. This approach can be very valuable when large amounts of data are being handled.

When performing internal data conversion of this type, structure and comment the code to prevent confusion by anyone working on the program at a later time.

Use bit packing — The C language allows the addressing of data at the bit level. This can provide large space savings if the data types allow bit packing. The things to look for are arrays of flags or counters with a limited range. These two types are easily translated into bit-level storage.

Use memory-efficient data structures — When the memory constraints are severe, all data structures must be examined in detail. Structures such as linked lists carry a cost for their convenience. In some cases it may be necessary to resort to more primitive data structures in order to save the memory used by the pointers that serve as the links in the list. In some cases the memory overhead for linked data structures can be severe. However, the code to manage the more primitive data structures will also use some memory. Consider these options carefully.

13.4 SPEED CONSIDERATIONS

There are times when speed is the key consideration for a program. In these cases the optimization considerations are different from when memory is the main consideration. When working on speed problems, it is important to install performance indicators so improvements can be verified. The indicators may be as simple as repeating a segment of code a large number of times and timing the execution. Here are some points to consider when working on speed problems.

Locate the key areas — In most programs, a very small portion of the code is responsible for most of the time-critical operation. The first task is to determine what code is being executed when speed is required. Remember that speed is rarely required for the whole program.

Function calls cost — In key areas it may be useful to pull function code into the mainstream to avoid the overhead of the function call and return. This is especially true of calls to small functions. The use of macros to contain the code can make this less messy than it may seem, but remember that you have removed the data separation that comes with call-by-value.

Loops cost — Are all of the loops in the key code necessary? If a loop is executing a small segment of code only a few times, it may be worth expanding it. Also, consider having loops which count up to some value count down to zero instead. This can make for a shorter compare at the end of the loop, since most computers have hardware instructions for comparing a value with zero.

Calculate constants outside of loops — Never calculate constants inside a loop. For example:

```
while(. . . . .){
    x = y1 * sin(33.0/57.2958);
    }
```

should be changed to

```
sin1 = sin(33.0/57.2958);
while(. . . . .){
    x = y1 * sin1;
    }
```

or even

```
#define SIN1 .04391    /* sin of 33 degrees */
  while(. . . . .){
    x = y1 * SIN1;
    }
```

This simple change can often cut the run time of a loop by 90% or more, since calculations take much longer than the simple loop control structures.

Use the shortest data type — If an **int** or an **unsigned** will do the job, don't use a **long**. However, it usually isn't worth doing pre- and post-conversion of data if the object is to increase the speed of the program.

Consider the data structures — When looking at ways to save memory, we mentioned downgrading linked lists to arrays. When speed is the primary concern, think about going the other way. If the data is to be sorted, inserted, or deleted many times, it may be faster to upgrade arrays, or parallel arrays, to linked lists.

Use register variables — Choose the most active variables for register variables. Look for variables which are accessed many times, such as an inner loop index.

13.5 SUMMARY

This chapter has listed some methods that may make your program more efficient. These are separated into memory conservation methods and speed increase methods. The memory conservation methods are:

1. Clean up any inefficiencies in the program.
2. Search for blocks of common code.
3. Utilize register variables.
4. Use small data types.
5. Consider data type conversion and use the smallest possible types.
6. Pack bits.
7. Use memory efficient data structures even if they require some extra manipulation.

The speed increase methods and considerations are:

1. Locate the key areas and concentrate there.
2. Remember that function calls cost.
3. Loops also cost.
4. Calculate constants outside of loops.
5. Use the shortest data type.
6. Consider the data structures and use the one requiring the least manipulation.
7. Use register variables.

Test each of the techniques on your own system to see the true savings.

PROGRAMMING EXERCISES

1. We wish to investigate the memory cost of using automatic variables versus the cost of using register variables. Enter the following four programs on your system and compile them. Compare the size of the object files. What does this tell you about the use of register variables?

   Program 1

   ```
   main()
   {
       int x;
   }
   ```

   Program 2

   ```
   main()
   {
       register int x;
   }
   ```

   Program 3

   ```
   main()
   {
       int x;
       x++;
       x += x;
       x * = x;
       for(x=0;x<10;x++);
   }
   ```

Program 4

```
main()
{
    register int x;
    x++;
    x += x;
    x * = x;
    for(x=0;x<10;x++);
}
```

2. Repeat the experiment from Exercise 1, but compare long versus short variables rather than register versus automatic variables.
3. Test the following program on your system. Adjust the constant **LIMIT** so you can time the various loops accurately.

```
#define LIMIT 50
#define SIN2 .04391

#include <math.h>
main()
{
    float x,y,sin1;
    int i,j;
    y=1.1;
    x=y*sin(33.0/57.2958);
    printf("start test 1\n");
    for(i=1;i<LIMIT;i++){
        for(j=1;j<100;j++){
            x=y*sin(33.0/57.2958);
            }
        }
    printf("End test 1\n");
    delay();
    printf("start test 2\n");
    sin1=sin(33.0/57.2958);
    for(i=1;i<LIMIT;i++){
        for(j=1;j<100;j++){
            x=y*sin1;
            }
        }

    printf("End test 2\n");
    delay();
```

continued

```
        printf("start test 3\n");
        for(i=1;i<LIMIT;i++){
            for(j=1;j<100;j++){
                x=y*SIN2;
                }
            }
        printf("Test complete\n");
        }
delay()
{
    int i,j;
    for(i=1;i<1000;i++)for(j=1;j<1000;j++);
    }
```

4. Try the following program on your system. Replace the "beeps" with more elegant solutions, like the exact time. The constant **TIMELOOP** should be adjusted to have the program run for a reasonable time, like 30 seconds.

```
#define TIMELOOP 5000001
/*
    This program is a crude speed test to compare
    the speed of count up loops with count down to
    zero loops.
*/
void main()
{
    int j;
    long i;
    printf("\n Get ready\n");
    for(i=1;i<TIMELOOP;i++)for(j=1;j<10;j++);
    printf("\n start \n");
    beep();
    i=j=0;
    for(i=1;i<TIMELOOP;i++){
        for(j=1;j<5;j++);
        }
    beep();
    printf("\n part 1 complete\n");
    printf("\nA brief delay loop.\n");
    for(i=1;i<1000001;i++) for(j=1;j<10;j++);
    printf("\n start part 2\n");
    beep();
    i=j=0;
    for(i=1;i<TIMELOOP;i++){
        for(j=4;j>0;j--);
        }
    beep();
    printf("\n part 2 complete\n");

    }
```

5. Enter the three programs below and perform timing tests. The results will give you an idea of the speed differential between loops and repetitive code. What is the effect of using a register variable for the inner loop index in the third program?

Program 1 — code repeated five times — no loop

```
#define TIMELOOP 60000
main()
{
    int i = 0;
    int index;
    for(index=0;index<TIMELOOP;index++){
        calcsq(i++);
        calcsq(i++);
        calcsq(i++);
        calcsq(i++);
        calcsq(i++);
    }
}
calcsq(i)
int i;
{
    i *= i;
}
```

Program 2 — loop instead of repeated calls

```
#define TIMELOOP 60000
main()
{
    int i;
    int index;
    for(index=0;index<TIMELOOP;index++){
        for(i=0;i<5;i++){
            calcsq(i);
        }
    }
}
calcsq(i)
int i;
{
    i *= i;
}
```

Program 3 — loop with register index instead of repeated calls

```
#define TIMELOOP 60000
main()
{
    register int i;
    int index;
    for(index=0;index<TIMELOOP;index++) {
        for(i=0;i<5;i++){
            calcsq(i);
        }
    }
}
calcsq(i)
int i;
{
    i *= i;
}
```

Appendices

OPERATOR PRECEDENCE

The table on the following pages lists all the operators used in C in their order of precedence. When two operations are contained in the same statement, the one with the higher precedence will be performed first. For example, in

    a = b + c * d + e

the operation **c*d** will be performed before the addition statements because * has higher precedence than + . This is the same as

    a = b + (c*d) + e

Note that operations are always performed in the innermost level of parentheses first because parentheses have the highest precedence.

In the following table operators with equal precedence are grouped together. Associativity is left/right except for the second group (unary operators), and the assignment operators.

Operator	Description
()	function call or grouping
[]	element of an array
.	structure member
->	structure member where pointer is used to address structure
!	logical not (i.e., !x is "not x")
~	one's complement
-	minus, when used to negate a variable (a = -b)
+ +	increment
--	decrement
&	address
*	indirection - use variable as pointer
sizeof	returns number of bytes of variable
(type)	changes type of variable
*	multiply
/	divide
%	modulus
+	addition
-	subtraction
< <	left-shift bits
> >	right-shift bits
<	less than
>	greater than
< =	less than or equal
> =	greater than or equal
= =	equal (relational comparison, not assignment)
! =	not equal
&	and bits
^	exclusive or-bits
¦	or bits

continued

Operator	Description
&&	logical and
¦ ¦	logical or
? :	conditional assignment *ternary operator*
=	assignment (also + = , * = , etc.)
,	separator for multiple expressions

Associativity is left/right except for the second group (unary operators), and the assignment operators.

Appendix

B

ASCII CONVERSION CHART

Decimal	Octal	Hex	C Code	ASCII
0	0	0	\0	nul
1	1	1	\1	soh
2	2	2	\2	stx
3	3	3	\3	etx
4	4	4	\4	eot
5	5	5	\5	enq
6	6	6	\6	ack
7	7	7	\7	bel
8	10	8	\b	bs
9	11	9	\t	ht
10	12	A	\n	nl
11	13	B	\v	vt
12	14	C	\f	ff
13	15	D	\13	cr
14	16	E	\14	so

continued

Decimal	Octal	Hex	C Code	ASCII
15	17	F	\15	si
16	20	10	\16	dle
17	21	11	\17	dc1
18	22	12	\18	dc2
19	23	13	\19	dc3
20	24	14	\20	dc4
21	25	15	\21	nak
22	26	16	\22	syn
23	27	17	\23	etb
24	30	18	\24	can
25	31	19	\25	em
26	32	1A	\26	sub
27	33	1B	\27	esc
28	34	1C	\28	fs
29	35	1D	\29	gs
30	36	1E	\30	rs
31	37	1F	\31	us
32	40	20	\32	space
33	41	21	!	!
34	42	22	\''	''
35	43	23	#	#
36	44	24	$	$
37	45	25	%	%
38	46	26	&	&
39	47	27	\'	'
40	50	28	(	(
41	51	29	)	)
42	52	2A	*	*
43	53	2B	+	+
44	54	2C	,	,
45	55	2D	-	-
46	56	2E	.	.
47	57	2F	/	/
48	60	30	0	0
49	61	31	1	1
50	62	32	2	2
51	63	33	3	3

continued

Decimal	Octal	Hex	C Code	ASCII
52	64	34	4	4
53	65	35	5	5
54	66	36	6	6
55	67	37	7	7
56	70	38	8	8
57	71	39	9	9
58	72	3A	:	:
59	73	3B	;	;
60	74	3C	<	<
61	75	3D	=	=
62	76	3E	>	>
63	77	3F	?	?
64	100	40	@	@
65	101	41	A	A
66	102	42	B	B
67	103	43	C	C
68	104	44	D	D
69	105	45	E	E
70	106	46	F	F
71	107	47	G	G
72	110	48	H	H
73	111	49	I	I
74	112	4A	J	J
75	113	4B	K	K
76	114	4C	L	L
77	115	4D	M	M
78	116	4E	N	N
79	117	4F	0	0
80	120	50	P	P
81	121	51	Q	Q
82	122	52	R	R
83	123	53	S	S
84	124	54	T	T
85	125	55	U	U
86	126	56	V	V
87	127	57	W	W
88	130	58	X	X
89	131	59	Y	Y
90	132	5A	Z	Z

continued

Decimal	Octal	Hex	C Code	ASCII
91	133	5B	[	
92	134	5C	\\	\
93	135	5D	]	]
94	136	5E	^	^
95	137	5F	_	_
96	140	60	'	'
97	141	61	a	a
98	142	62	b	b
99	143	63	c	c
100	144	64	d	d
101	145	65	e	e
102	146	66	f	f
103	147	67	g	g
104	150	68	h	h
105	151	69	i	i
106	152	6A	j	j
107	153	6B	k	k
108	154	6C	l	l
109	155	6D	m	m
110	156	6E	n	n
111	157	6F	o	o
112	160	70	p	p
113	161	71	q	q
114	162	72	r	r
115	163	73	s	s
116	164	74	t	t
117	165	75	u	u
118	166	76	v	v
119	167	77	w	w
120	170	78	x	x
121	171	79	y	y
122	172	7A	z	z
123	173	7B	{	{
124	174	7C	|	|
125	175	7D	}	}
126	176	7E	~	~
127	177	7F	?	del

Appendix

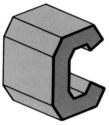

BASE
CONVERSION
CHART

Decimal	Binary	Octal	Hex
1	0000000000000001	000001	0001
2	0000000000000010	000002	0002
3	0000000000000011	000003	0003
4	0000000000000100	000004	0004
5	0000000000000101	000005	0005
6	0000000000000110	000006	0006
7	0000000000000111	000007	0007
8	0000000000001000	000010	0008
9	0000000000001001	000011	0009
10	0000000000001010	000012	000A
11	0000000000001011	000013	000B
12	0000000000001100	000014	000C
13	0000000000001101	000015	000D
14	0000000000001110	000016	000E

continued

Decimal	Binary	Octal	Hex
15	0000000000001111	000017	000F
16	0000000000010000	000020	0010
32	0000000000100000	000040	0020
64	0000000001000000	000100	0040
128	0000000010000000	000200	0080
256	0000000100000000	000400	0100
512	0000001000000000	001000	0200
1024	0000010000000000	002000	0400
2048	0000100000000000	004000	0800
4096	0001000000000000	010000	1000
8192	0010000000000000	020000	2000
16384	0100000000000000	040000	4000
65535	1111111111111111	17777	FFFF

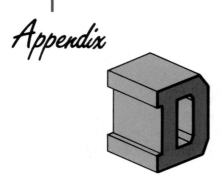

Appendix D

DEVELOPMENT
SUPPORT
PROGRAMS

LINT — A C PROGRAM CHECKER

Most C development systems include a version of the **lint** program which is used to check program source for errors and constructions which will compile, but may cause execution errors. Some of the errors checked for by **lint** are:

1. Unused variables and functions.
2. Unreachable statements.
3. Infinite loops.
4. Inconsistent type usage.
5. Unused and mismatched returns.
6. Syntax which limits portability.

The **lint** program is invoked by

lint [options] main.c sub1.c sub2.c

where **main.c**, **sub1.c**, and **sub2.c** are all parts of the same program.

The options are used to suppress the standard types of error checking and to invoke other checks. The **XENIX** version of **lint** includes the following options:

–a	Suppress complaints about assignments of type **long** to variables that are not of type **long**.
–b	Suppress complaints about unreachable **break** statements.
–c	Suppress complaints about casts that may limit portability.
–h	Suppress application of heuristic tests for execution bugs.
–u	Suppress complaints about undefined functions and external variables.
–v	Suppress complaints about unused arguments in functions.
–x	Suppress complaints about variables declared as **external** and never used.
–n	Suppress compatibility checks against the standard or portable **lint** library.
–p	Attempt to check for portability.
–l**library**	Check function definitions in the specified library.

These options are specific to the **XENIX** version of **lint**, but similar options (or the very same ones) will be available for the **lint** program on your system. It is strongly suggested that you use **lint** during the development of large programs.

CB — A C PROGRAM PRINT BEAUTIFIER

Most C development systems include a copy of **cprint**, or a similar program which is used to produce listings that are more easily readable than printouts of the source files. The usual invocation is:

cb main.c

which will produce a file, **main.lst**, with the beautified listing. For example, the following source:

```
main()
{
    int height,vel=0,damping=2;
    int acc=-1;

    printf("Enter the integer starting height. ");
    scanf("%d",&height);
    while(height>0 || vel !=0){       /* as long as we are not at rest */
```

```
            printit(height);
            height=height+vel;
            vel+=acc;
            if(height<=0){
                vel=(-damping)-vel;
                if(vel<0)vel=0;
                height=0;
                }

        }
    }
printit(hgt)
int hgt;
{
    int x;
    for(x=1;x<hgt;x++)printf(" ");
    printf("X\n");
    }
```

was processed using a MS-DOS print beautifier to produce

```
BALL.LST   File: 18 Jul 1987  2:34pm  Listing: 18 Jul 1987  2:37pm


main()
{
    int height,vel=0,damping=2;
    int acc=-1;
    printf("Enter the integer starting height. ");
    scanf("%d",&height);
    while(height>0 || vel !=0){        /* as long as we are not at rest */
  ^     printit(height);
  ^     height=height+vel;
  ^     vel+=acc;
  ^     if(height<=0){
  ^     |   vel=(-damping)-vel;
  ^     |   if(vel<0)vel=0;
  ^     |   height=0;
  ^     }
  ^
    }
}
printit(hgt)
int hgt;
{
    int x;
    for(x=1;x<hgt;x++)printf(" ");
    printf("X\n");
}
```

If the second listing is preferable to you, use the **cb** program, or the equivalent program on your system.

RETAB – A PROGRAM REFORMATTER

As programs get modified, the indentation often becomes wrong due to the addition or deletion of loops and conditionals. At this point a large amount of effort may be required to make the indentation match the structure of the program. Many development systems contain a **retab** program to fix the indentation of the source. This program is invoked by

    retab main.c

This program produces a reformatted source file in **main.c** and most versions produce a backup file.

Appendix

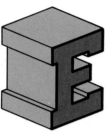

XENIX INCLUDE FILES

The following is a sampling of the include files provided by XENIX. There are other include files supplied, but this is a good representative sampling.

curses.h — A collection of cursor control functions.

dial.h — Defines communication functions for XENIX communications.

fcntl.h — Defines values for file control functions.

lockcmn.h — Defines the locks for file control.

macros.h — Defines string handling and other useful macros.

malloc.h — Defines the routines **malloc**, **free**, **realloc**, **mallopt**, and **mallinfo**.

math.h — Defines the math routines **atof**, **frexp**, **ldexp**, **modf**, **erf**, **erfc**, **exp**, **log**, **log10**, **pow**, **sqrt**, **floor**, **ceil**, **fmod**, **fabs**, **gamma**, **hypot**, **matherr**, **sinh**, **cosh**, **tanh**, **sin**, **cos**, **tan**, **acos**, **atan**, **atan2**, **j0**, **j1**, **y0**, **y1**, **yn**, and **asin**.

stdio.h — Provides the standard definitions necessary for I/O. This also defines the I/O macros.

string.h — Provides the definitions necessary for string manipulation functions.

ascii.h — Defines the standard ASCII names.

Appendix

COMPILER
INFORMATION

NOTE: The following information is specific to the XENIX system and C compiler. Check with your system reference manual if you have any problems with these options. Similar options are available for most C compilers.

C COMPILER OPTIONS

−c	Create object modules, but do not invoke the linker.
−CSOFF	Turns off subexpression optimization. This is valid with the −O option only.
−CSON	Turns on subexpression optimization. This is valid with the −O option only.
−d	Print a trace to tell on which pass the compiler is.
−Fxxxx	Set the size of the program stack to **xxxx**. On AT class machines the default is 2000. The number **xxxx** is in hex.
−Fa[file]	Create an assembly listing of the program and put it in **file**. If **file** is not specified, the listing is placed in file **source.s**.

–Fc[file]	Create a combination source and assembly listing in **file**. The assembly listing is interleaved with the C source listing. If **file** is not specified, the listing is made to file **source.l**.
–Fl[file]	Create a combination assembly and object code listing in **file**. If **file** is not specified, the listing is made to file **source.l**.
–Fm[file]	Produce a load map listing and place it in **file**.
–Fs[file]	Create a source code listing and place it in **file**.
–Ipath	Add **path** to the list of searched directories for include files.
–lfile	Tells the linker to search **file** for unresolved references. The **file** must be a legal library that has been processed through **ranlib**.
–LARGE	Create a large model object file.
–ofile	Tells the linker to put the executable code in **file**. If this is not specified, the executable file is **a.out**.
–O	Turns on code optimization.
–w	Suppresses warning messages from the compiler. If you need this option, you should reexamine your code.

Appendix

G

ANSWERS TO ODD-NUMBERED QUESTIONS

CHAPTER 1 — QUESTIONS

1. Why are programs in C memory-efficient?

   C programs are memory-efficient because the language structure is simple and the run-time system is very small.

3. Why is speed of compilation important?

   During development a program will be compiled many times. The compile time is a major portion of the overall development time of a program.

5. What is a function library?

   A function library is a collection of C functions, which are similar to Pascal procedures or FORTRAN subroutines.

7. What are some of the sources of function libraries?

   They can be written especially for an application, written as a utility library, purchased from companies that specialize in utility libraries, or they may come with the compiler.

9. What can be said about a language that does not allow the assignment of a floating-point number to an integer variable?

   That it is strongly typed.

11. Is C a strongly-typed language?

    No. The code:

    ```
    int x;
    char ch;
    x = ch;
    ```

    is legal in C.

13. Is it generally faster to write a program in a high-level language or in assembly language?

    The development time for high-level languages is generally much shorter than the development time for a similar program written in assembly language.

15. BASIC is supplied with most MS-DOS systems. What is the major difference between this version of BASIC and a language like C or Pascal?

    BASIC is an interpretive language, not a compiled language. This means the program is read and executed one line at a time.

17. Does C support modular programming?

    Yes.

19. If routines are compiled separately, how are they put together to be used?

    The linker puts together object modules. The linker can be called explicitly, or a combination of source and object files can be specified to the compiler.

CHAPTER 2 — QUESTIONS

1. What is the basic function of the C compiler?

   The C compiler translates the text of the program into object code.

3. What is the traditional file extension for a source file under UNIX (or MS-DOS for that matter)?

   .c

5. What is the default executable file name produced by the linker under UNIX?

   a.out

7. Can the compile and the link steps be combined?

   They usually are. You must use the –c option to stop the linking.

9. If the compiler detects fatal errors, is the linker invoked?

   No.

11. Does the compiler or the linker detect undefined functions?

    The linker.

13. What error does the linker produce if the same function is defined twice in a program?

    Duplicate function definition. The action taken by the linker is machine dependent. The linker may ignore the second definition, or stop the linking process.

15. How often should you back up your source files?

    Once a day on micros, and before making major program structure changes on all machines.

17. What is the purpose of the **–c** option on the compiler call?

    The –c means compile only, do not invoke the linker.

19. What is the purpose of file **math.h**?

    This file contains all necessary definitions for using the math functions.

CHAPTER 3 — QUESTIONS

1. What does the **#** character in column 1 signify?

   The # in column 1 signifies a preprocessor command.

3. Can variables be declared outside a function boundary?

   Yes, but they are not owned by any function. This can be dangerous if different functions change the same variable.

5. What characters are used to delimit a block of code?

   {   }

7. Can a statement be more than one line in length?

   Yes. The only part of the source that cannot be split is text within quotes.

9. What does the **%d** code specify in the **printf** control string?

   The %d specifies that the associated variable should be printed in integer format.

11. What is the purpose of the %c code inside a control string?

    The %c specifies a character be printed.

13. What do the following character strings represent?

    a. \n   **new line**

    b. \''   **''**

    c. \'   **'**

    d. \65   **ASCII 65 or the letter A**

15. What does the **#include** statement do?

#include adds read the specified file during the compile cycle.

17. What is the purpose of indenting code?

To make the program more readable.

19. How many lines in length can a comment be?

There is no limit.

21. Describe the quickest way to comment out a block of code.

Add a /* at the beginning of the block and a */ at the end of the block.

23. What does the preprocessor do?

It reads the source code, expands macros, and processes the preprocessor commands directed to it.

25. How many arguments are required when calling a function?

None.

27. What is the significance of the name **main** for a function?

The function main is passed control when the program is executed.

29. What is the purpose of the function **strcmp**?

strcmp compares strings.

CHAPTER 4 — QUESTIONS

1. What are the four data classes in C?

auto, external, register, and static.

3. What is the abbreviation used for declaring a variable external?

extern

5. What are the three basic data types?

int, char, and float.

7. Express the groups of statements below in a more compact form.

  a. int x;
     int y;
     int x,y;

  b. int x;
     x = 3;
     int x = 3;

  c. x = 0;
     y = 0;
     x = y = 0;

  d. x = x + y;
     x + = y;

  e. int x,y;
     x = y − (y/10)∗10;
     x = y % 10;

  f. x = x + 1;
     x + + ;

  g. x + = 1;
     x + + ;

  h. y = x;
     −−x;
     y = x−−;

9. What are the variations that can be added to the basic data types?

long, short, double, and unsigned.

11. How do you insure that a constant is of type float?

    Use a decimal point (i.e., 3.0 instead of just 3).

13. What is suspicious about the following statement?

    if(x = y)plotx();

    The conditional form of the equality check is = = not = . The above statement does an assignment inside the if statement.

15. What is wrong with the following sequence?

    int x[20];
    x[20] = 5;

    The array contains 20 elements, 0,1,2,3 ...19. There is no x[20].

17. What is the final value of **x** in the sequence below?

x = (y = (z = 2;	**x = 2 y = 2 z = 2**
z = Y-- * x;	**z = 4 y = 1 z = 4**
x = (x != y) ? z : y;	**(if x ! = y)x = z;**
	else x = y;

    4

19. Which of the following are reserved words in C?

    The reserved words are boldfaced.

    a. double
    b. then
    c. while
    d. basic
    e. real
    f. rand
    g. auto
    h. entry
    i. DEFAULT

21. Is the following expression true or false?

    ((3>2)&&(3<3))||(4==5)||((3>2)&&<3==3))

    (T && F) || F || (T && T)
    F || F || T
    T

23. What is TRUE defined as?

    1

25. What is the significance of the character '\0'?

    This is the end-of-string specifier.

27. List the six relational operators.

    = =   >   <   < =   > =   ! =

29. Why would the variable name milestotal be preferable to the name totalmiles?

    Try to avoid starting names with words like total, because if the number of significant characters is less than the word that starts the name, the names totalmiles and totalcars will be considered the same variable. Most compilers recognize at least eight characters. XENIX recognizes 31.

CHAPTER 5 — QUESTIONS

1. What are the decimal values of the following constants?

    a. 023   **19**
    b. 077   **63**
    c. 0x34   **52**
    d. 010000   **4096**
    e. 0x10000   **65536**
    f. 03007   **1543**
    g. 0xFFFF   **65535**
    h. 077777   **32767**

3. How many bits are required to store the number 74,234?

    17

5. What are the results of the following calculations?

    a. 0x55 & 0x33
       0x11

b. 0x55 ¦ 0x33
   0x77

c. 170 & 0x77
   0x22 or 34

d. 033 + 05
   040

e. 'A' ˄ 0x20
   'a'

f. 'a' ˄ 040
   !

g. (0x07 < <1) & 0x0D
   0x0D

h. 0x01 < <7
   0x80

i. (0x33 < <4) > >4
   0x33

7. What is the C symbol for the OR operator?

   ¦

9. Upon which data types can Boolean operations be performed?

   int and long

11. What is the ~ operator?

   one's complement

13. How many meaningful bits are there in a type char?

   usually 8

15. Which bit is the sign-bit in a 16-bit integer?

   bit 15

17. How is a negative number represented in a signed integer?

   By setting all high-order bits to 1.

19. If the result of the operation

    number & 1

    is nonzero, what do you know about the value of the variable **number**?

    It is an odd number.

21. What operation can be used to perform the converse of the operation in Question 14?

    number & = ~1;

23. How many bits are in a char variable?

    8

25. Do bit fields increase memory requirements in a program?

    No, they usually reduce memory requirements.

27. How will memory be allocated in bit fields?

    On word boundaries.

29. Which of the following statements contain errors?

    a. x & = 0x3f
    b. y < = 3
    c. x ^ = 0xf0
    d. **x~ = 0x0a**   **This equals x = x ~ 0x0a and ~ is a unary operator. It does not accept 2 arguments.**
    e. **x ¦¦ = 0x20**   **The ¦¦ operator is a conditional. This is not illegal, but it doesn't make sense.**

CHAPTER 6 — QUESTIONS

1. Which of the following statements is legal?

    The boldfaced statements are correct, the incorrect portions of the others are underlined.

    a. **if(a = = b)printf("Hello");**
    b. if(a = = b){ printf("Hello")}   **No ; (after closing)**
    c. **if(a = = b) { printf("Hello");}**
    d. **if(a)printf("Hello");**

  e. **if(a = = b)printf("hello);**
      else printf("Goodbye");
  f. **if(a = = b ¦¦ a>b)printf("Hello);**
  g. **if(a ¦¦ b)printf("Hello);**
  h. **if(a && b)printf("Hello);**

3. What will be printed in the following sequence?

```
x=1;
y=2;
if(x==y)printf("ABC");
else printf("DEF");
```

DEF

5. Are the following code segments operationally equivalent?

Segment 1:
```
        if(a==b)printf("Hello);
```
Segment 2:
```
        if(a==b){
            printf("Hello");
            }
```

YES

7. What is wrong with the following sequence?

```
if(maximum == 0){
     minimum =0;
     }
median=(maximum-minimum)/2;
else {
     minimum = maximum/2;
     }
```

The if and the else are separated by a statement.

9. What is the function of the **default** when used with a **switch** statement?

Control is passed to the default when none of the other cases are true.

11. Can more than one **case** be used for the same block of code? For example:

```
case 'A'
case 'a'
     printf("Choice is A");
     break;
```

YES

13. What will be printed in the following sequence?

```
x=3;
switch(x){
     case 1:
     case 2:
          printf("X<3\n");
     case 3:
          printf("X=3\n");
     case 4:
     case 5:
          printf("X>3\n");
     default:
          printf("X unknown\n");
     }
```

X = 3
X > 3
X unknown

This is because there are no break statements separating the blocks of code.

15. Can the following example be rewritten with a **case** statement? Explain.

```
int x,z;
x=getnumber()
if(x == z)functn1();
else if(x == z*2)functn2();
else if(x == z*3)functn3();
else if(x == z*4)functn4();
else error();
```

No. The switch/case tests a variable against constants.

17. Which C loop structures check the condition before executing the statement contained inside the loop?

for and while

19. Can there be a reason for having a **while** statement with a null statement?

Yes, often the important code is contained inside the while conditional statement.

21. How many of the components of a **for** statement are required?

None, the statement for(;;;) is legal.

23. What are the uses of the following loop?

```
for(;;;){
  some code in here
        }
```

This is an infinite loop. There are some cases when this is useful.

25. What is wrong with the following code sequence?

```
do{
        printf("Looping\n");
        x++;
        }
printf("At end of loop");
while(x<10);
```

The variable x is not initialized.

27. What do the **break, continue,** and **goto** statements have in common?

They are all varieties of jumps, and tend to undermine structured code.

29. What are the usual reasons for resorting to **goto** statements?

Usually laziness. There are some conditions when gotos are useful, but usually the code can be better structured to remove the need.

CHAPTER 7 — QUESTIONS

1. What is the relationship between pointers and addresses?

Pointers are addresses.

3. What is the **&** operator used for?

The & returns the address of a variable.

5. What is the indirection operator, ∗, used for?

Accessing variables through a pointer.

7. How is an array declared?

Using the square brackets, [], to specify the number of elements (i.e., int x[20];).

9. What is the first element of an array in C?

Element 0.

11. What is the difference between a pointer constant and a regular pointer?

A pointer constant cannot be changed.

13. What is the relationship between arrays and pointers?

The C language converts array notation to pointer notation internally.

15. Can multiplication be performed on pointers?

Yes, but it doesn't yield useful results.

17. What is the resulting value printed out after this sequence of code?

```
int arr[20];
int i;
int *px,*py;
for(i=0;i<20;i++)arr[i]=i;
px=&arr[5];
py=&(*px);
printf("Value in py = %d.\n",*py);
```

5

19. What is the data type of the variable **name** in the following declaration?

char **name;

It is a pointer to a pointer to a character.

21. Which of the following code segments are legal, but are probably not doing what the programmer intended?

The questionable segments are in boldface type with explanations following.

a. int *pointer
    int x;
    float y;
    pointer = &x;
    pointer++;

This leaves an integer pointer pointing to a type float (y).

b. int *pointer
    int x[10];

```
float y;
pointer = &x;
pointer += 2;
```

The result of multiplying a pointer by 2 is not the same as multiplying the index by 2.

c. ```
int *pointer
int x[10];
float y;
pointer = &x;
pointer += 5;
```

**This sequence is ok.**

d. ```
int *pointer
int x[10];
float y;
pointer = &x;
pointer += 10;
```

This leaves a pointer pointing to the 11th element of an array dimensioned to 10.

23. What is the effect of the double indirection operator (**)?

This gives you a pointer to a pointer. This is useful when using arrays of pointers.

25. What is the instruction that will increment the fifth character of the string pointed to by the second element of array x?

```
x[1][4]++;
```

27. Does C monitor the array indices during run time?

No, so if there is a problem you can easily crash your program.

29. Can pointers be used to address hard-coded memory locations?

Yes. The pointer can be set to a constant if the memory location is known. This is a common way of interfacing with hardware.

CHAPTER 8 — QUESTIONS

1. What is the error in the code on the following page?

```
main()
{
   char *bufptr;
   getline(bufptr);
}

getline(buffer)
char *buffer;
{
   scanf("%s",buffer);
}
```

No storage was ever set aside for the data, only pointers were defined.

3. What values can be returned by a function of type **void**?

    None.

5. What is the relationship between parameter declarations and the parameter list?

    They must match.

7. What separates the parameter declarations and the function code?

    The initial { of the function.

9. What is the relationship between a function's type and the value returned by the function?

    They must be of the same data type.

11. Can a function return without a **return** statement?

    Yes, by "falling off the end."

13. What type of argument is associated with each the following format specifiers for function **printf**?

    a. %s   ***char**
    b. %c   **char**
    c. %d   **int**
    d. %f   **float**

15. Is C a call-by-reference or a call-by-value language?

    Call-by-reference.

17. What is the danger of call-by-reference?

The called function can change the variable passed to it. This can cause problems if the calling function did not expect the variable to be changed.

19. What are the disadvantages of using externals?

Lack of control over the variables. Using externals is not a structured programming technique.

21. What is recursion?

A function which calls itself is called recursive.

23. Are there cases where a function's recursive call to itself is not conditional?

There should not be.

25. Where are external variables first declared? Which declaration creates storage for the variable?

External variable storage is created by declaring the variables, without the external identifier, outside of any function.

27. Why is it better to place any external variable definitions in an include file?

That way when changes are made, it is insured that all functions accessing those variables will have the changed definitions.

29. Where are **argv** and **argc** initialized?

The system initializes them at start-up.

CHAPTER 9 — QUESTIONS

1. What are the advantages of using **typedef** statements?

Flexibility and clarity.

3. The **FILE** type is created by a **typedef** in **stdio.h**. What is the definition of a **FILE** type?

It is a structure that varies from system to system. Look at the stdio.h file on your system.

5. Is the following statement legal?

   typedef char;

   No, there is no type defined.

7. What is the type of **house.color** in the following example?

   ```
   struct{
       char *type;
       char *location;
       int size;
       int color;
       }house;
   ```

   int.

9. What data type is **ourcar** in the following sequence?

   ```
   struct car{
       char *model;
       int year;
       char *color;
       };
   struct car *ourcar;
   ```

   ourcar is a pointer to a car structure.

11. What will be printed in the following sequence?

   ```
   struct car{
       char *model;
       int year;
       char *color;
       }lotcars[20];
   struct car *ourcar;

   for(i=1;i<20;i++){
       lotcars[i].year=65+i;
       }
   ourcar=&lotcars[0];
   printf("The answer is %d.",ourcar->year);
   ```

   65

13. Is the following sequence correct?

   ```
   typedef struct{
       char *model;
       int year;
       char *color;
       }CAR;
   CAR lotcars[20];
   ```

Yes, the type CAR is defined as a structure.

15. What is wrong with the following sequence?

```
struct car{
    char *model;
    int year;
    char *color;
    struct car lotcars[10];
    };
```

The structure contains itself. This is an infinitely recursive definition.

17. Comment on the legality of the following sequence.

```
struct car{
    char *model;
    int year;
    char *color;
    struct car *oldcar;
    }ourcar;
struct car lotcars[20];

ourcar = lotcars[10];
ourcar.oldcar=&ourcar;
```

It is legal if the compiler supports structure assignment.

19. What is the alternative to using the -> operator?

Instead of cat->dog, you can use (*cat).dog.

21. What is a union?

A union is a type of structure where storage is only allocated for the largest of the elements defined.

23. How do you know what data type is stored in a union variable?

It is your responsibility to keep track of what data type is stored in a union.

25. What is the **enum** declaration used for?

Declaring an enumeration type. This sets up enumeration constants and variables.

27. What is wrong with the following sequence?

    ```
    enum color{red = 1, orange = 2, yellow = 3, green = 1,
        blue = 2, indigo = 5, violet = 6};
    ```

    The enumeration constants red and green have the same value.

29. What is the advantage of using enumeration types?

    It offers better readability and has the same advantages of typedef statements.

CHAPTER 10 — QUESTIONS

1. What is the difference between dynamic and standard memory allocation?

   Dynamic memory is not part of the program, but is requested from the system as needed.

3. What problems may occur with dynamic memory allocation?

   The system may not grant the memory request.

5. What is the function **sizeof** used for?

   To determine the size of a variable. The size of a variable is needed if memory is to be requested for it.

7. Can a stack be split among multiple memory segments?

   No.

9. Are stacks an example of FIFO, or LIFO, storage?

   LIFO.

11. What condition indicates that a stack is full?

    top-bottom = size of stack

13. What condition indicates that a circular buffer is empty?

    in = out

15. What is the major disadvantage of linked lists?

    The memory required for the links.

17. What is garbage collection?

Aggregating small pieces of memory freed by data deletes or moves into usable blocks.

19. Name three examples of data structures that can be easily represented with trees.

Family trees, Bill of Materials, Decision trees.

CHAPTER 11 — QUESTIONS

1. Which of the following **printf** statements contain errors?

The statements with errors are in boldface type.

a. printf("This is a good line.");
b. **printf("Charlie said, "This is a good line".");**
c. printf("Donna said, \"This is a good line.\"");
d. **printf("There are %d cars in the system.",&cars);**
e. **printf("Change your directory to \%d.",dirnum);**
f. printf("%d\% of the cars are missing.",miscars);
g. **printf("The cost is $1.2d.",cost);**
h. **printf("The company spent $%d% of its income.");**

3. Given the declarations

```
int number;
float temperature;
char string[20];
```

which of the following **scanf** statements contain errors?

The statements with errors are in boldface type.

a. **scanf("%s %d",string,number)**
b. **scanf("%s, %d,string,number);**
c. **scanf("%s%d",string,number);**
d. **scanf("%s %d",&string,number);**
e. scanf("%s,%d",&string[1],&number);
f. **scanf("%4.6f",temperature);**
g. **scanf("%4.6",&temperature);**
h. scanf("%4.6f",&temperature);

5. What value does the **fopen** function return when a file cannot be opened?

   NULL

7. Is the **fclose** function needed before an **exit**?

   No.

9. What is the difference between the **strcpy** and the **strcat** function?

   strcpy copies, strcat concatenates strings.

11. What type is the function that must be provided to compare values for the **qsort** function?

   int

13. What is the range of values checked for by the following functions. (For example, **isdigit** checks for characters 0–9.)

   a. isalpha   **a–z and A–Z**
   b. isupper   **A–Z**
   c. islower   **a–z**
   d. isalnum   **a–z, A–Z, and 0–9**
   e. isascii   **0–127**

15. What type is the function **ftell**?

   long

17. What type is the function **malloc**?

   ***char**

19. One of the arguments to the function qsort is a function. What is its purpose?

   To perform the compare of the two variables.

INDEX

, , 283

! = , 62, 70, 282

#, 38
#define, 37
#include, 160

%, 59, 69

&, 82, 128, 129, 282
&&, 63, 283

*, 69, 128, 129, 282

+, 69, 282
+ +, 60, 69, 282

__, 60, 282
/, 69, 282

<, 62, 70, 282
< <, 85, 282
< =, 62, 70, 282

=, 56, 283
= =, 62, 70, 282

>, 62, 70, 180, 282
> =, 62, 70, 282
> >, 85, 282

?, 67
?:, 70, 283

\'', 43
\0, 43

^ XOR, 82

{, 34
}, 34

¦, 82
¦ ¦, 63, 283

~, 86, 282

A.out, 21
Addition operator, 69
Address operator, 66, 128
Addresses, 127
AND, 82
ANSI standards, xvi
Argc, 160, 161
Arguments
  command line, 160
  function, 152
Argv, 161
Arrays
  character, 64
  definition, 130
  indexes, 130
  initialization, 65
  multidimensional, 137
  notation, 134
  of pointers, 137
  of structures, 177
  parallel, 173
  pointers to, 130
  strings, 64
ASCII, 43, 54, 58, 285
Ascii.h, 295
Assignment of structures, 178
Assignment statements, 56
Auto, 52
Automatic storage class, 52